INTERIOR DECORATING

A Reflection
of the
Creator's
Design

BETHANY HOUSE
PUBLISHERS
MINNEAPOLIS, MN 55438

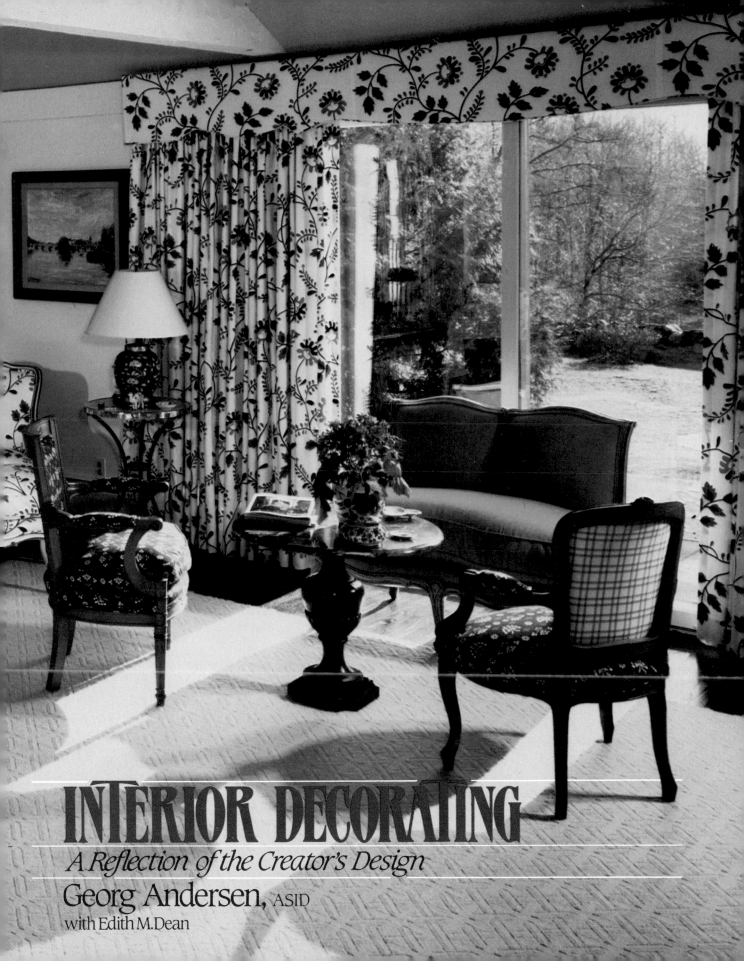

INTERIOR DECORATING

A Reflection of the Creator's Design

Georg Andersen, ASID

with Edith M. Dean

Dedication:

To Annabelle Andersen and Jim Dean
who so graciously and helpfully put up
with Georg and Edith while they worked
on this manuscript.

Interior Decorating—A Reflection of the Creator's Design
Georg Andersen and Edith Dean
ISBN 0-87123-288-X
Copyright © 1983
Georg Andersen
All Rights Reserved
Published by Bethany House Publishers
A Division of Bethany Fellowship, Inc.
6820 Auto Club Road, Minneapolis, Minnesota 55438
Design by Koechel/Peterson Design, Minneapolis
Printed in the United States of America

CONTENTS

A Note from the Authors

Our primary purpose in writing this book is to point out ways we can use our homes to glorify God. It is our sincere hope that you will implement the suggestions contained here to challenge yourself—as these ideas have challenged us—and to help others.

Foreword

What a joy it was when each of us, as very young children, first discovered that we could give our thoughts to those we loved by using *words*. Words were the tools we needed! How eagerly we worked at learning new ones so that we could communicate accurately what was in our hearts and minds!

Now that we are grown and have homes and families, we want to communicate in new ways to those who are special in our lives. One way we can reach out to those we meet is through our homes. That desire to reach out and touch is the central difference between a mere house and a home. But in order for our homes to speak the language of love and caring, we need to learn the "words."

Through the sensitive writing of Edith Dean, Georg Andersen becomes the master teacher in this lovely book. Dipping from his deep reservoir of professional experience, he freely pours out to us his secrets of interior design—the tools (the words) we need for expressing what we desire to say with our homes. Harmony, tranquillity, joy, peace, humor, comfort, caring—all these we long to communicate, both to our own families and to our friends.

In a day when, in most houses, nobody's present, and when all too many youngsters feel more "at home" in the video arcade than they do in their mother's kitchen, I believe Christians will welcome these practical suggestions for making home look like a place where somebody cares—and a place where the family chooses to stay.

As we use this book and its suggestions, I pray that each of us will keep always in mind that these decorating secrets are only the "words." The message has to come from deep inside our hearts, from a firm commitment to make our homes more than a place to sleep and bathe. May our decorating be merely the words we use to say to all who enter our homes, "You are loved!"

Gloria Gaither

Meet Georg Andersen, ASID, Your Interior Designer

I first met Georg Andersen by telephone in November 1980. This man's voice alone swiftly convinced me of his integrity, his quiet confidence and his positive approach to his profession—and to life itself.

Later I learned that two years before this, in October 1978, Georg, who then lived in New York, had noted on his desk calendar that he someday would write a book about interior design from a Christian viewpoint. At that time I was living in Los Angeles. Eventually both of us had moved (the Andersens in January 1979; the Deans in May 1980) to the beautiful little Arkansas town of Conway. In February 1981, Georg and I began working together on the writing of this book.

Georg Andersen is an internationally known architectural/interior designer. His ASID affiliation indicates that he has been certified by the American Society of Interior Designers.

Because God has gifted and blessed him in his field of interior design, Georg believes God desires that he share his talent, skill, knowledge and experience with you and other Christians. He knows that your surroundings *do* affect you—your activities; the degree of your enthusiasm for life; even your spiritual, mental and physical health. Georg will lead you through the pages of this book toward an affordable interior design that can help you toward peace—with yourself, with your fellowman, and ultimately, with God.

Georg often refers to a quote from the late A. W. Tozer: "First, He created for utility and purpose and then added decoration and beauty. There probably is a sense in which we could get along without decoration, but it is better to have it. There is that which is in the mind of God that desires to be pleased—not only satisfied. Order and usefulness and purpose bring satisfaction, but God desired that there should be beauty in His work." Georg Andersen believes this can be true of your home.

Perhaps the interior design of your home is almost what you want; perhaps you, like many people, know good design when you see it, but you don't know what makes it good. Whichever your situation, you need the approval, direction or advice of an expert. Wherever you are on the economic scale, whether you must monitor every penny or can afford to splurge, if pleasant, practical, attractive living quarters are your goal, Georg Andersen can help you.

Starting with an impressive educational background, Georg built an equally impressive professional career. In 1961, he was graduated from Parsons School of Design in New York with a degree in Interior and Architectural Design, subjects he later taught there. He also studied at L'ecole D'Architecture in Fountainbleau, France, on an ASID scholarship. His commercial clients include Revlon, Bristol Myers Company, Phelps Dodge Corporation, and the Waldorf Astoria Hotel in New York. His residential clients include many corporate heads of the Fortune 500 companies. His designs are featured every two years in the Ethan Allen Treasury Catalog. His work has been published in all major interior and design publications, including *Architectural Digest* and *Interior Design.*

Several years ago, while head of Georg Andersen Associates, Inc., on Madison Avenue in New York, he realized that he was spending too many hours in the office. He knew that God wanted him to give his family priority over his business affairs. So he prayed for guidance. This resulted in the Andersens' move to Arkansas where he is president of the Little Rock firm of Cromwell Interior Design, Inc. Visiting in their new home in Arkansas, one can feel the pervasive contentment that has come to the Andersen family.

Besides his qualifications as an interior designer, Georg, first of all, understands people. Friendly and confident, he has a particular ability to appraise a person's priorities and life-style, and give proper decorating guidelines. From his years of experience in working with people, he has anticipated many of your questions and provided the answers in this book.

Second, he has great respect for an individual's personal memories. He knows that, in the proper setting, people will be happier with familiar furnishings, especially those that have been rubbed and worn and loved into a satiny mellowness. He knows, too, that God created us as unique individuals. Therefore, the "look" he creates is that of the individual family—not of Georg Andersen. "My greatest compliment," he notes, "comes from the client who says, 'My house looks like me.'"

Third, he is considerate of one's budget, large or small. He will find innovative ways to make each well-loved item a client owns contribute to an overall plan of good design. No, Georg is not the kind of designer who suggests that you discard everything you have and start over. His philosophy is that your home should express *your* personality, not his. This is why, with a little common sense, and with principles and suggestions found in this book, you will be able to decorate your home successfully.

As a Christian, Georg asks: "How can I be the best steward of my time? Of my abilities? Of my finances? Of my home? Since all these things belong to God, how does He want me to use them?" This man, who personally practices careful budgeting so that he can give to others who may need financial help and who frequently reassesses his role as a Christian steward, willingly gives devotion to a God who desires it, but who does not demand it.

This book is an outgrowth of that devotion. You will become aware of Georg's urgency to share all the gifts God has given him. You will understand that here is a man who seeks and uses God's limitless ability as he leads you in planning and implementing the interior design of your home.

Edith M. Dean

The exterior of the Andersen home, Higher Ground.

CHAPTER ONE

YOUR HOME: A SANCTUARY

The beauty of the house is order;
The blessing of the house is contentment;
The glory of the house is hospitality;
The crown of the house is godliness.

Fireplace Motto/Author unknown

The most important quality of the home has very little to do with interior design. The home first must be a God-ordained sanctuary for family and guests, a place on which, and in which, God confers His presence and love. Only then can interior design fulfill its highest purpose—reflecting God's design.

Home is the most important thing in your life, next to your family and your body. The common belief that the one who lives in a luxurious house is more richly blessed than the one who lives in, for instance, a furnished room is not necessarily true. Any place can be a home. Material possessions in themselves do not bring loving friends and relatives, or physical, mental and spiritual health. Alcoholism, marriage rifts and parent-child conflicts occur in the homes of the wealthy and in the homes of the poor.

Here are five questions I sometimes use to check my home's "condition": When my doorbell rings, does my house echo my greeting, "Welcome—come in and sit down"? Does it offer a place of contentment, tranquil-

lity, edification, and sturdy affection? Do my children like to bring their friends home? Is it my church away from church? *Does it glorify God?*

Your home should, and can, do all these things. With today's social pressures on your family, it is more important than ever that your house exude order, hospitality, contentment and godliness. Whether your family is gathered as a unit or whether your guests number one, a dozen, or more, each occupant should feel reluctant to leave.

Perhaps you have experienced leaving a home in which precision prevailed over love. If so, you undoubtedly felt like an intruder while you were there and left feeling very depressed. Or perhaps you have visited a home where, amid a bit of comfortable clutter, you felt accepted and you experienced a holy sense of calmness, serenity and joy. Orderliness in the home is a plus as long as it is tempered with reason.

The most attractively designed home in the world is not guaranteed to bring you happiness

unless you are happy within yourself. Embarrassment, on the one hand, or a healthy pride regarding your home, on the other, has no relationship to your income group or age. I've seen both attitudes among young and old, whether they are wealthy, middle income, or poor. But there is no reason to be ashamed of your home as long as it is as clean and as attractive as you can make it at the moment. This is where I think I can help you.

Good interior design gives a feeling of solidarity, coupled with imagination and a definite expression of one's personality. However, good design also shows good judgment in that it does not offend the sensibilities of others. But one's personality must first be put in order. With the Psalmist we cry, *"Create in me a clean heart, O God, and renew a right spirit within me"* (Psalm 51:10). *God* is the one who is able to restore order in our personalities. Then we are able to set our minds on things that are *"true...honest...just... pure...lovely...of good report..."* (Phil. 4:8).

For a Christian, good interior design should reflect a heart in harmony with the Spirit of God.

Then our lives and homes can be filled with *"love, joy, peace, longsuffering, gentleness, goodness, faith, meekness, temperance..."* (Gal. 5:22-23). For a Christian, good interior design should reflect a heart in harmony with the Spirit of God. Personally, I gain much guidance in this matter from Psalm 1:1,2—*"...But his delight is in the law of the Lord; and in his law doth he meditate day and night."*

Interior design also can change and restore troubled emotions. I am convinced that good interior design does contribute to contentment and fullness of joy. I have seen both qualities conceived in formerly wretched people as I began to redesign their homes; I have watched both qualities grow almost apace with my progress.

A very special case was that of a family of dear friends who attended our former church. Their teenaged daughter was in the youth group that my wife, Annabelle, and I sponsored.

The family's problems had come on gradually. When they first bailed their son out of drug-related trouble with the police, like all parents, they must have thought it would never happen again. But it did happen again—and again—and again. Our friends were distressed and grieved, and they were spending all their resources—time, energy and finances—trying to restore their wayward son.

My wife, Annabelle, and I knew they were having problems when we saw how they were neglecting their home. After several years of continuing anguish and heartbreak, the parents were too wearied to notice the threadbare carpet, the peeling paint, the sagging curtains, or the worn and fading sofas and chairs.

Because the teenaged daughter did not want to be reminded of the situation, she spent much of her time away from home. When she did go home, she tried to stay alone in her room or bury her head in a book. The home's state of disrepair had become too painful for her. Both daughter and parents were embarrassed to invite friends in, so, in spite of a horrible sense of guilt, they did not reciprocate invitations they received. Soon their social contacts had all but dwindled to nothing.

Annabelle and I recognized their problem as a vicious circle that continued to turn out more and more negative results.

At this time, God had especially blessed our own business and finances. After prayer and meditation, we knew we were to take positive action and pass these blessings on to our distraught friends. We knew, too, that we could not give our money without giving ourselves. So we completely redesigned the entrance area to their home, their living room and their dining room.

The excitement of sparkling clean rooms, refurnished and trimmed in vibrant blues, greens and crisp whites, was contagious. It revived in our friends their former emotional balance, their self-confidence, and it even helped to restore their faith in the Lord. I am reminded again of David's prayer, *"Create in me a clean heart, O God; and renew a right spirit within me"* (Ps. 51:10). That *"right spirit"* was renewed within our friends almost instantaneously. Even so, they admitted to a small case of nerves when they invited us to their home for supper one Sunday evening after church. "It has been a long time," they told us, "since we have felt the desire or the freedom to invite friends into our home."

Their son, now happily married, is no longer on drugs. The daughter has graduated from college. And our friends are now joyously at work on the mission field.

I make no claim that the redesign of their home solved their problems, but it did help to draw their attention away from their seemingly hopeless situation and be able to reach out for help and healing. They sensed that God, through others, did care about them. So the interior-design work, in results that they could both see and feel, was obviously the catalyst that turned them back in the right direction.

This is why we believe in the importance of interior design— because it reflects God's creativity and order, and because it helps create an atmosphere in which people can know, and become like, Him. John Ruskin, nineteenth-century English critic, said, "This is the true nature of our home—it is the place of peace, the shelter not only from all injury but from all terror, doubt, and division." And it matters not whether you live in a mobile home, an apartment, a cottage or a mansion, your home should be a dwelling place of God.

"This is the true nature of our home— it is the place of peace, the shelter not only from all injury but from all terror, doubt, and division."

What could have been an awkward jog in the Andersen living room became a cozy corner, a sanctuary for relaxing with family, friends, or for being alone in unhurried communion with God.

CHAPTER TWO

WHERE SHOULD YOU START?

"By wisdom a house is built, and by understanding it is established; and by knowledge the rooms are filled...."

Proverbs 24:3, 4

Many of us need to overcome the impatience that makes us unwilling to start where we are; rather than making gradual changes, we think that we must have a house completely decorated to our taste before we can truly begin to "live." We spend a great deal of pace-the-floor time between our decision to redesign our homes and the day our efforts have reached fruition. Actually, this transition period will be no great problem *if* we continue to enjoy and to invite friends into our homes while the planning and work progress.

One of my client families proved the value of doing this. They knew their home did not reflect their true personalities, but they were content with what they had until desired changes could be made.

On my first visit to their home, I was greeted at the door by an energetic, middle-aged woman, with blonde hair and sparkling eyes. She led me into an atmosphere of pristine, off-white walls, where formality and a certain aloofness were provided by silk curtains and sofa coverings. Very beautiful objects of art—such as an intricately

carved coral statue sheltered in a lighted glass vitrine and excellent examples of Chinese porcelains riding on top of the breakfront—were kept far from the reach of hand or eye. The family and their friends could not really enjoy their beauty. Fortunately, this vivacious lady had refused to allow her rather solemn house to stifle her personality.

As a general premise, it is often the case that happy, sparkling people choose bright colors and that quiet, contemplative people prefer neutrals—but not always. Through interior design, many people with varying personalities and tastes are able to respond favorably to a wide spectrum of colors.

I certainly am not a psychologist, but it seems to me that some quiet, retiring people I have known are not truly so by nature, but their personalities have been subdued by force of circumstances. I believe that some in this group can be helped toward freedom in expressing themselves more honestly through the use of warm,

bright colors in their environment. On the other hand, some of the gentlest people I know are able to live with strong, rich, dark colors, including liberal amounts of black, without feeling overwhelmed by it.

All that is to say that color can be used to express a certain type of nature, to bring a measure of release to one who is unduly reserved, or can help to "round out" a particularly unique personality.

Before I can help my clients, I must come to know them. Back to the case in point, I learned that this was a second marriage for my vivacious lady client and her husband, and that the house had been decorated to match the personality of the former wife. He was aware of the need for a change, especially since this was now home to combination families of six lively youngsters.

With merely a few modifications, a few touches here and there, and at minimal expense, I was able to turn the stiff formality of the living room and the bedrooms into something more casual, more in keeping with the family's effervescent spirit. Silk damask yielded to colorful, snappy cotton and linen prints in curtains, sofas, chairs, and throw pillows. Seating groups were rearranged for conversational comfort (see pages 44 through 51 for various seating groupings). Now removed from its vitrine, the carved coral statue, as well as other art objects, disseminate their special beauty throughout the house. Primitives have replaced the more formal paintings by the masters, and a natural-colored, fringed, knotted-linen rug covers the floor instead of the heavy Oriental.

As I progressed, my clients spent no thumbs-twiddling time. They continued their "business-as-usual" hospitality, and they became obviously more happy, more alive, and more "at home" in their new "this-is-for-us" atmosphere.

As you work toward the redesigning of your home, there are certain guidelines you should observe in order to discover what is "right" for you. As you begin, be assured that the Lord truly cares about your particular environment, that He wants you to be relaxed and happy in your home, and that He will help you to use your home as a spiritual retreat center for family and friends. You can ask for and receive His help as you work out an individual, overall plan. You will start to experience the step-by-step thrills of implementing the interior design of your home.

STEP ONE

Do what I ask all of my clients to do: Begin a collection of pictures, cutting out interiors you like from magazines such as *Architectural Digest, Better Homes and Gardens, Family Circle, House Beautiful, Ladies' Home Journal, Woman's Day*— or from some of your own favorite magazines.

Save only pictures which appeal to you at *first glance*. Do *not* study them; your feelings about color, style, arrangement, furnishings should *not* be analyzed yet. Put them in a folder until you have accumulated forty or fifty. This could take several weeks—but be patient! You've accepted the interior-design challenge. You're on your way.

STEP TWO

After completing your collection, open the folder and begin to analyze the pictures. What at-a-glance features persuaded you to retain each picture? What similarities kept recurring? Make notes in answer to these questions, then group the photos according to the patterns that have developed. Notice an emerging *color pattern* (blue rooms with white rugs, red rooms with white rugs, etc.). Notice the *background materials and their coloring* (wood paneling, ceiling beams, stone or wood flooring, cream walls). Notice *upholstery style and coverings* (soft and inviting with lots of pillows, or dignified with formal sofas and chairs). Notice *fabrics* (plaids, white linens, splashy floral prints). Now you are beginning to know what you actually prefer. (An actual case history appears in Appendix A, page 114.)

STEP THREE

You should now take inventory of the furniture, accessories and works of art you already own. Make a room-by-room listing of furnishings, their colors and their sizes (dimensions are as important as color). This listing will help you later when you

consider rearranging furniture or perhaps when moving to a new home. It is easy to overestimate or underestimate the size of furnishings to which you've become accustomed. You may think a table you've owned for years is 36 inches in diameter and therefore limited in its functions. But after measuring it, you may find it is only 20 inches, exactly right for the lamp table you need in the entrance area.

Although good interior design need not be expensive, I must concede that good quality almost always is. Design and quality are often considered twins, but they are not of the Siamese connection. You can sense "design" at first contact, but the longer you own and live with a piece of quality furniture, the more you will appreciate the care and artistry that was put into it. Cabinetry is an art form that is as respected as that of the great master painters. The English respected their cabinetmakers enough to name furniture after them. They came close to revering Thomas Chippendale, who worked almost exclusively in mahogany. His most famous creation was the camel-back sofa. As you work toward your interior-design goal, you will find the distance between design and quality being somewhat reduced.

You have now taken steps to discover what colors, materials and styles best express your personality. Don't be discouraged if everything is not clearly delineated in your mind. More will "fall into place" as we continue our discovery of the best interior design for your family.

Your list of furnishings is another step toward your goal of a warm, comfortable, inviting home. Your first goal-step, of course, is the collection of from 40 to 50 pictures of rooms as suggested earlier in this chapter. From these, you should be discovering and affirming what you really like. The second goal-step is acquiring a preliminary knowledge of good interior design. As we move into Chapter Three, you will find a great deal of information on this. It will also explain the value of a swatch-board and how to set one up. Thus, individual goal-steps will take you through the book until you reach Chapter Ten, *Before You Go Shopping.* Your interior-design plan for your home is "growing"—at a pace with your new understanding of your own preferences within the parameters of your budget.

CHAPTER THREE

BASIC PRINCIPLES OF DESIGN

*"God's fingers can touch nothing
but to mold it into loveliness."*

George MacDonald

During your phase of collecting photographs, there will be times of waiting until you reach your goal of forty or fifty. During the phase of analyzing these photos, there will be times when you should lay aside the pictures in order to get a fresh perspective. You must necessarily wait for results from both phases before you can begin to use your room inventories. These pauses are a good time to acquire a preliminary knowledge of basic principles of design.

Color

Color is the most effective and exciting of all decorating elements. If dark ones are used, the room appears smaller; if pale, the room appears larger. Because colors are affected by their neighbors, they can, if poorly planned, snarl and clash. Properly used, however, color creates an aura of warmth, vitality and beauty. Look around you at the artistry of God—the vibrant colors He uses in a rainbow, the aurora borealis, the Painted Desert, a dawn or a sunset. Know by these that you should not be timid about using *any* of His colors.

Color seems to assume a major role in bringing a sense of contentment to the room. It makes the first and most lasting impression when a person enters it. It creates a mood: gaiety, tranquillity, drama, subtlety. And it evokes an emotional response.

In 1938, quite inadvertently, Dr. Lillian Ray Titcomb proved that we are all affected by color. It was then she persuaded her sorority, the Delta Gamma Alumnae of Southern California, to help her start the Blind Children's Center in Los Angeles for the preschool blind.

She told about the blind children's inexplicable fascination with color. It was virtually impossible to explain color to a child who had never seen daylight. Even so, almost every day Dr. Titcomb was asked questions about color: "What color dress do you have on, Doctor?"

"I have on a blue dress."

"Oh. Blue is nice. I do like blue."

Next day: "What color dress are you wearing today, Doctor?"

"I'm wearing a red dress."

"Oh. Red is beautiful."

Next day: "What color is your dress today, Doctor?"

"Brown. I have on a brown dress today."

"Ugh. I don't like brown."

If color evokes such a sharp response from sightless, preschool children, think what it can do for those of us who do see.

Before making any color decisions, check several paint chips in the lighting of your home to see if they are compatible with your carpet and other furnishings. Remember that the color on the painted wall will not match that on the paint chip. To see the on-the-wall color, *fold* the paint chip into itself— the color in the crease is the color that will appear on your walls. If, for some reason, you are not able to use this test, choose a lighter shade than that on the paint chip.

COLOR WHEEL

The color wheel is used to determine which groups of colors contrast and which harmonize. Related colors are positioned next to one another, contrasting—or complementary—colors are opposite (for example, warm reds, oranges, and yellows face their complements, the cool blues, greens, and violets). The primary and secondary colors compose the basic color spectrum, and addition of the tertiary colors completes the standard color wheel shown here. All of these colors, though foundational, represent the merest fraction of a nearly infinite variety of color gradations.

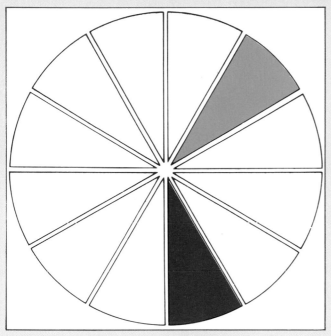

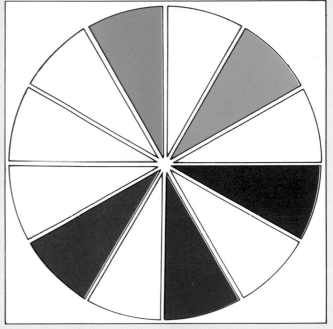

Primary colors: red, yellow, and blue. These colors are pure; they cannot be created by mixing any other colors, but all other colors are formulated by mixing these. Combined in equal amounts, red, yellow, and blue create gray.

Secondary colors: orange, green, and violet. These are created by mixing two primary colors (for example, red combined with an equal amount of yellow creates orange). Each is the complementary color of the one primary color not used.

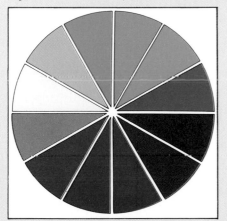

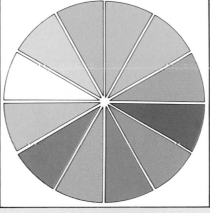

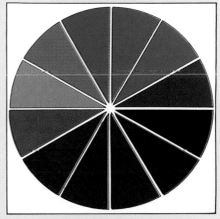

Tertiary colors: These are created by combining a primary and the secondary next to it (for example, red mixed with its neighbor, orange, creates the tertiary red-orange).

Tints: colors with white added. Here, 50-percent white has been added to the standard color wheel. *All* of the lightened colors harmonize.

Shades: colors with black added. In this case, 50-percent black has been added to the standard color wheel.

You should settle on *one* color as a common denominator throughout your house.

You should settle on *one* color as a common denominator throughout your house. The more you repeat that color, the more you will add to the rhythmic flow of your home and the larger it will seem. You can use a deeper shade of your color in small accent doses or larger amounts of it in paler shades.

One of today's prominent colors is neutra, a neutral beige, also called putty. It is a gray beige with no pink and it has several advantages:

1. Most people react positively to it.
2. It "likes" so many colors. Against it
   a. Crisp, clean whites are very white.
   b. Coral is very pristine.

An excellent combination is a neutra-colored carpet with walls two shades lighter, baseboards in white with a ceiling of robin's egg (or bristol) blue.

Color can be used, also, as a camouflage. Suppose, for instance, that you have a carpet in good condition but that it is a pink beige, which disturbs you. Negate some of the pink by painting the walls a complementary color, say, a gray beige. If, on the other hand, the beige in the carpet is too gray, add pink to the beige in the wall paint. These are optical illusions, to be sure, but the important consideration is that the pink—or the gray—is no longer disturbing.

Complementary colors often can be used in this fashion. The two most prominent pairs are red and its complement, green; blue and its complement, orange. The color wheel on page 19 further describes this phenomenon.

Terra cotta is another color used widely, especially in carpeting. It is remarkably like a pale rust and is beautiful with crisp, white curtains.

Today we are amazed that blue and green were considered for many years a strange combination, although they so aptly represent God's growing things and His sky. With them, too, you can use a myriad of colors: lavender, yellow, pink, etc. However, every room needs some white to "split" and define colors, thus lessening chances for color clash.

If you have a green carpet with walls two or three shades lighter, you may want to try white in curtains and upholstery. Green-and-white plaid, or a floral pattern are adaptable to almost any room. Leaf or fern prints can be used with florals but don't try to put more than one floral print in the same room—leave this to the experts.

Where possible, let your colors spring from patterns in your rug. This creates unity and gives your rug proper consideration as another work of art.

The swatchboard

The best interior-design tool for gaining a good perspective of your overall work is the swatchboard—one for each room you redesign. To be effective, it should contain samples of *all* the materials you will use. It is very important that the size of each sample be in proportion to the area of each room it will represent, as in the drawing below (also see Photo on p. 22).

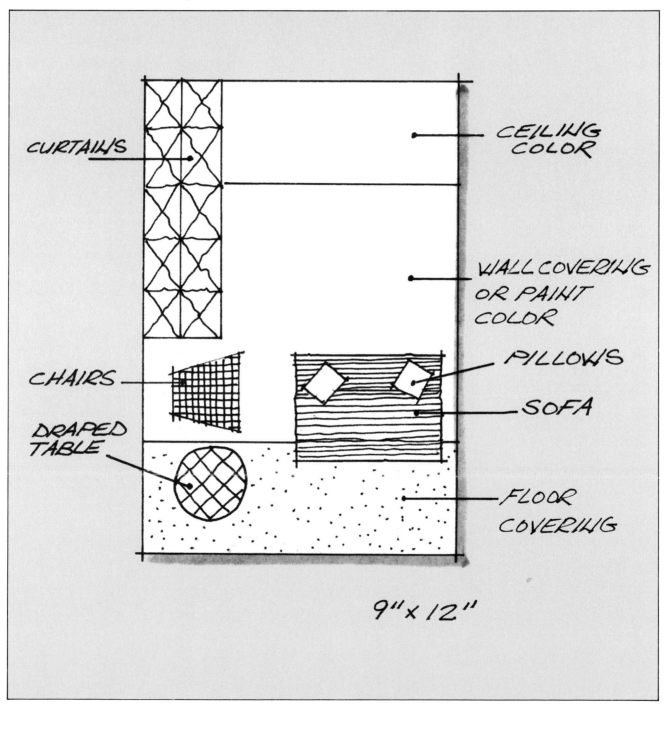

CURTAINS

CEILING COLOR

WALL COVERING OR PAINT COLOR

PILLOWS

CHAIRS

SOFA

DRAPED TABLE

FLOOR COVERING

9" x 12"

A typical layout for a swatchboard.

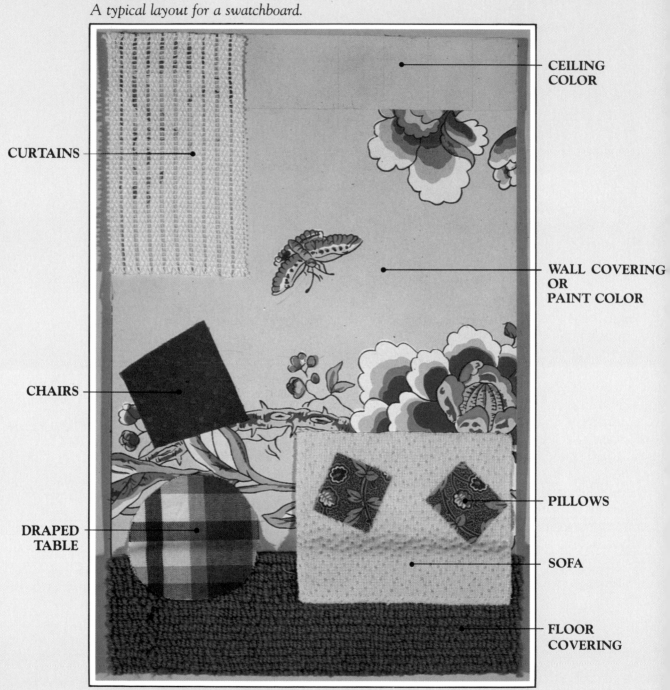

CEILING
COLOR

CURTAINS

WALL COVERING
OR
PAINT COLOR

CHAIRS

PILLOWS

DRAPED
TABLE

SOFA

FLOOR
COVERING

*This Photo and the Drawing on
page 21 should be viewed as a
single unit. It is important that
each swatch sample be in proportion to the area of the room it
represents.*

Before mounting the swatches, place all of the samples on a table. Mix, match, and discard until you are pleased with your choices. Once you have made up your mind, *don't compromise.* If you have decided on lemon-yellow throw pillows, don't settle for a butter yellow.

A 9" × 12" manila file folder makes an excellent swatch-board. Not only is it easily carried as you shop for the materials, but it is handily filed away for use later when you desire replacement materials or household linens.

Where do you get swatches for your board? Most upholstery shops, carpet and linoleum stores, paint and wallpaper stores will help you find scraps, but you may have to make several trips to find what you really want. As for fabrics, some designers will let you check through their older books. At times, it may be necessary to buy small pieces of fabrics. Obviously, this is less expensive than buying the full quantity, only to find later that the fabric does not coordinate well with other material you have selected.

It is not wise to discuss swatchboard progress with your relatives or friends until you have a choice of arrangements from which they may select their favorite. Aunt Mamie will say, "It's okay, dear, I suppose—only..." Uncle Charlie will think everything is great, "—but isn't the wallpaper a little—well, you know, loud?" Cousin Gertie will say, "It's simply darling—but do you *really* like that shade of blue?"

To avoid such "compliments" that may cause you to doubt your own choices, show the swatchboard arrangements only to family members who live in your home.

Mix, match, and discard until you are pleased with your choices. Once you have made up your mind, *don't compromise.*

Art

Art is nearly as personal as your toothbrush (if *you* like it, be it landscape or seascape, impressionistic or modern, it's good), so I never dictate its selection to my clients. If requested, I will point them to a school of painting or a particular artist.

Hanging pictures

There are not many picture-hanging rules I adhere to, but the following are helpful, even though they may take a bit of getting used to:

1. Vertical paintings and framed mirrors enhance a room because the vertical look is architecturally more pleasing than the horizontal look. The vertical look helps to give the room a feeling of height, "lifting" the ceiling.

Since vertical paintings are difficult to find, a clear, simply framed mirror is much more attractive and often less expensive than a poorly executed painting.

To achieve a good working proportion, use paintings or mirrors 3 feet wide by 4 feet high in rooms with a standard 8-foot ceiling. This suggestion will aid you in becoming sensitive to good proportion.

A single painting usually should be hung at eye level, which means the center of the picture will be 5'6" from the floor. If you are hanging one over a table or credenza, 8" to 12" above is your guideline.

2. It is better to separate two equally proportioned pictures. Hang one on each of two walls or one on either side of a larger mirror or related picture.

3. You may hang one equally proportioned picture above another.

4. Odd numbers of equally proportioned pictures hanging side-by-side give great visual pleasure.

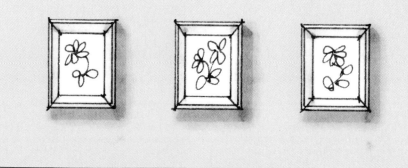

5. When hanging pictures, one above the other (which I find very engaging), hang the larger above the smaller.

6. Do not hang two equally proportioned pictures side by side. Your eyes will get confused and, instead of looking at either picture, will tend to look between them at what is known as a "style space."

7. Do not "stair-step" pictures. Not only is this an awkward arrangement, but your eyes will tend to climb steps rather than enjoy the pictures.

8. Hanging pictures from 10 inches below the ceiling to 24 inches off the floor, in this manner, can be very pleasing and gives a strong vertical line.

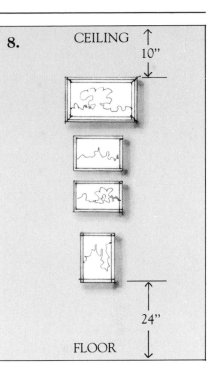

9. Surrounding a tall piece of furniture with related photographs or pictures can help to create a striking focal point.

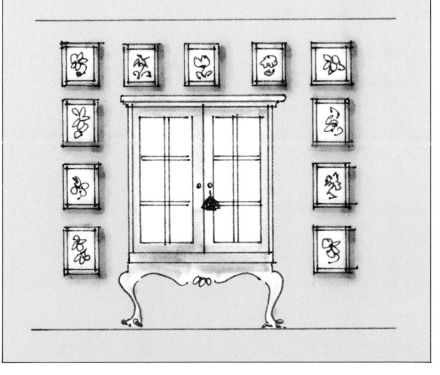

Paneling

Frequently I am asked to redesign owner-paneled rooms, which often are quite dismal and dark, especially if the paneling is of an inferior quality. To replace the "trailer syndrome" in these rooms—even if it *is* in a mobile home—with the effect of added texture, I encourage my clients to paint the paneling with a low-luster enamel as I have done in my own home. My family room and my children's rooms are painted white and the entrance area is painted yellow over paneling.

I have even at times advised my clients to panel a room for the sole purpose of painting over it. This gives a very handsome Early American or Country French character to the room. One can buy slightly damaged paneling at a reduced price. If the vertical grooves in the sheets of paneling are uniform, the finish is not important since it will be covered with the desired paint color.

It is rare that I encourage what is called an accent wall painted in a contrasting color. However, if you have a room with one paneled wall and the other walls are plain sheet rock, it is quite attractive to paint the paneled wall in a startling strong and wonderful color, such as raspberry red, navy blue, or bottle green and have the other walls be white. This establishes a warm focal point from which seating groups can spring. We will elaborate on this in Chapter Six.

Photos of the Andersen children hang on either side of an armoire in their family room. Topped off by attractive baskets, the armoire becomes a striking focal point.

If privacy is not necessary, window treatment should be uncluttered and "unfussy," exposing as much glass as possible.

Window treatment

There are only two good reasons for covering windows with curtains or blinds:

1. To screen an unsightly view.
2. To block out strong, hot sunlight (the eastern sun in the morning or the western sun in the afternoon).

If privacy is necessary, install a roller shade close to the glass at the top of the windows—preferably the plainest weave in a white, translucent vinyl shade; light will show through, images will not. If total blackout is desired, install white, totally opaque shades.

If privacy is not necessary, window treatment should be uncluttered and "unfussy," exposing as much glass as possible. To avoid the unpleasantness of black glass at night, use very fine-weave dacron draw curtains or roll-up/pull-up wooden or matchstick blinds. I prefer the narrow (Riviera) venetian blinds. Not only are they uncomplicated, but they are available in almost any department store. However, they are functional and contemporary and do *not* adapt well to period rooms.

Install floor-to-ceiling overcurtains (commonly called draperies) and undercurtains as near to the ceiling as possible. Even though you end up with a small space between the top of the curtains and the ceiling, this placement tends to heighten the room and is considerably more appealing than having the curtains drop from the tops of the windows.

Try hanging curtains on a wooden pole covered with a fabric identical to that of the curtains. If the fabric is printed, you may want to pull a contrasting color out of the print and cover the pole in a fabric of that color. Or paint the pole to match, or contrast with, the curtain fabric.

Often overcurtains that draw are a waste of money because

(1) They require that you purchase more fabric than you would otherwise.
(2) When opened, such curtains bunch together, thus covering any pattern.
(3) They do not fall properly.

For overcurtains, tightly woven fabrics are the most successful. Natural fabrics (cotton, linen, silk, wool) are preferable because they are easy to maintain. However, their high cost and, at times, their scarcity may preclude their use. And synthetic fabrics have been greatly improved through modern technology. If you must buy synthetics, take with you a small piece of the natural fabric you want to duplicate. Match the synthetic fabric as closely as possible to the natural.

Undercurtains are most successful in dacron-nylon, tightly woven, sheer fabric. Loosely woven sheers cause certain problems; they have a tendency to sag, they are affected by humidity, and they present a below-par appearance.

Whichever fabric you buy, have it professionally treated with Scotchgard. The treatment will more than pay for itself in lustrous appearance and in length of fabric life.

Within your color scheme, it is perfectly acceptable to mix fabric patterns in the same colors (e.g., blue-and-white polka dots, blue-and-white plaids, or blue-and-white crisscross). Even the straight lines of a plaid and the flowing lines of a floral have rapport if the pattern scale is similar and the colors are identical.

The front edges of the curtains can be trimmed with a contrasting color if you so desire. Almost any notions counter can supply bias tape, ¾ inch to 1 inch in width, for application to the front edge of the curtains. To dress up bed pillows, bedspreads and table accessories, you can also use rickrack or ribbons.

Usually valances should be avoided. Use them only if (1) you can afford to purchase pure silk tassel trim; (2) you can afford to have them installed properly by an expert; (3) you can afford the maintenance costs; and (4) you install them in a strictly period room.

Beautiful exterior plantings directly beyond windows can give ample privacy and eliminate the need for curtains. Black glass at night? Transform it into a beautifully dramatic scene by installing exterior floodlights directly beneath the windows and aiming them toward the plantings. During the winter when the lights play on God's evergreens and their twinkling snow-whiteness, this becomes a scene of breathtaking beauty (if, of course, you live in a northern clime). However, exterior lighting is effective only when interior lighting is kept very low.

Suppose you have an unsightly, badly proportioned window. Instead of blocking it off, attach a louvered shutter inside and paint the shutter and frame to match the wall. Watch that unsightliness disappear as the eye moves smoothly across the related colors and the louvered shutters provide both interest and daylight.

> Within your color scheme, it is perfectly acceptable to mix fabric patterns in the same colors.

Lighting

Lighting plays a major role in hospitality—even your porch light, which sends out a greeting to guests as they arrive, should be carefully chosen and placed. The most beautifully decorated room will fail to live up to its potential without good lighting. Although illumination is still the vital factor, lighting should also provide visual comfort. The combining of lighting and color is discussed later, room by room. A proper combination can enhance any mood you desire for yourself, your family and your guests.

Lighting on art

Picture lights mounted on paintings create a warmer and more intimate glow within the room than other forms of art lighting. To overcome their one disadvantage, the dangling cord, outlets should be installed directly behind the paintings, 5'6" from the floor to the center of the outlet.

Use only incandescent lighting for this purpose. Fluorescent lighting has the ability to change many hues completely; the blue of the light will drain color from a painting.

My personal collection of camels, most of which were gifts.

Floor covering

The ideal hardwood floor is stained a dark Tudor brown (by Minwax), and sealed with three coats of polyurethane in high gloss (my preference) or satin finish. But use dark colors only if the room is large.

In a contemporary scheme, have oak floors bleached professionally; industrial bleach is applied to take the red out of the wood, then albino bleaching stain by Minwax is applied and sealed with satin-finish polyurethane. Bleached wood floors are extremely pleasant. When used with light-colored walls, they leave no line of demarcation at the junction of walls and floors, and cause the entire space to appear larger.

Area rugs are always pleasing on hardwood floors. The rugs may be high- or low-textured, preferably in one color; they may be patterned, geometric (see Photo, p. 53—a reversible, wool dhurrie rug, also available in cotton), or floral (see Photo, p. 61—a reversible, wool Kilim rug). When an area rug is placed on a smooth wood floor, prevent its slipping and perhaps tripping someone by using a separate, thin (¼") rubber liner beneath it. If the liner is larger than the rug, simply trim the excess with household scissors.

If wall-to-wall carpeting is used, I advise against the use of thick rubber padding. I am aware that it makes a rug feel spongy and soft to walk on, but it will cause problems after a short period of normal use. The softer the padding, the easier it is for legs of chairs and tables to punch through the carpeting. A thin, dense, synthetic padding, or a hair-and-jute padding will add years to the life of your carpet.

It is wise to choose low-cut, pile fibers that have the appearance of wool. Such fibers will not show footprints, traffic patterns, or indentations where furniture has rested.

Types of rug fibers	
Wool:	most desirable and most expensive, abrasion- and soil-resistant, moderate-strength fibers.
Acrylan:	many of the same properties as wool in appearance, feel and resilience, but not as easy to clean.
Delustered nylon:	rather easy to maintain and, more importantly, does not have the sheen or stigma that nylon once had.

Whenever you see a well-designed interior, look at it carefully and ask yourself, "Why does this scheme 'work'?"

Review

As you walk the interior-design path, it is good to keep reviewing your original goals and objectives (it's necessary to look back to see whether you are climbing or descending). Admittedly, there may be times when you will feel like Walt Whitman's "patient, weaving spider," but, like that spider, you can succeed.

As with any skill, the more you practice your newfound insights of interior design, the easier they will be to use. Whenever you see a well-designed interior, look at it carefully and ask yourself, "Why does this scheme 'work'?" By doing this often, you will develop good judgment; and it will soon make itself evident—in *your* home.

Let's summarize briefly. As you have cut out and analyzed pictures as I recommended in Chapter Two, *Where Should You Start?*, you are discovering what specific architectural and design features you really like. This chapter, *Basic Principles of Design,* covered the use of color, the single most effective and exciting of all decorating tools. Proper hanging of paintings and mirrors were shown in captioned drawings. It also explained window treatments and various uses and types of paneling and floor covering.

You are learning about the colors and combinations you like and the ones you *don't* like. Before you start on your shopping trip, however, let's explore the interior design of the rooms in the following chapters.

CHAPTER FOUR

THE ENTRANCE AREA

"Welcome each other into your houses...."
1 Peter 4:9, Jerusalem Bible

The entrance area, or foyer, whether it is a hall or a direct entry into a room, should be especially charming because it gives the guest the first and most lasting impression of your home. In fact, this is the only area some visitors will ever see. Yet, most entrance areas are victims of neglect. They seem to be "tacked on" as an afterthought by both architects and designers.

I encourage my clients to "waste" space when planning and building their homes by making the entrance areas as large as possible—within reason, of course, and in keeping with the size of their homes. Because a small entrance area tends to make a large house appear smaller than it is and a large entrance area tends to make a small house appear larger, they are "wasting" space purposefully.

Keep in mind that your entrance area voices the all-important introduction to your home. Certainly you would never introduce two people this way: "You two have a great deal in common—Joe is a bird lover and Bill raises Maltese cats." Neither should the "introduction" to your home stand in open disagreement with the other rooms. Basically, all rooms, including foyer, should be decidedly neutral, or all should be decidedly colorful.

The entrance area should capture the essence of the design in your house. Since it is your basic color palette, even a neutral entrance area should provide glimpses of your favorite color—perhaps in the fabric covering a small stool, or in a bouquet of flowers (see Photo on p. 35).

If, however, your favorite colors are more vivid, you might use pineapple yellow walls with accents of other colors used elsewhere in the house, such as tangerine or apple green. To me,

nothing is more exciting than, as in music, a pianissimo start with a crescendo of vibrant colors that builds to a fortissimo. Such colors always need measured doses of white in woodwork and painted furniture. But how can a neutral scheme in the entrance of an otherwise colorful home be made to conform with the general, established palette? By including a painting or print that shows the stronger colors prevailing in the rest of the house.

An entrance area need not be painted. If you like flowers and floral prints, use a vine-patterned or latticework type of wall covering from which the floral prints in the rest of the house can spring. Thus, you, your family and your guests can walk through the promise of a flower garden to come.

If a coat closet is a part of the entrance, try a surprise. Paper its walls, ceiling, shelves, and the inside of the door with a small-patterned wallpaper.

Get as much natural light as possible into the entrance area. If you own your home, I encourage you to put glass in the front door, or side lights on either side. Through these at night, low-level illumination sends out a warm and cozy welcome. The preferred lighting is a lamp sitting on a chest or a table, but wall lights, such as sconces or glass lanterns are also good. Avoid ceiling (down) lights unless they are in combination with table or wall lights.

Although mirrors are rarely needed these days (few ladies wear hats anymore), they do give an illusion of space, for they reflect available light and beauty.

A hard floor is preferable in the entrance area. There are several types available.

Types of Entry Flooring	
Marble:	most expensive, durable, easily stained, hard to clean.
Ceramic tile:	durable, easy to maintain.
Vinyl tile:	most popular of resilient floor coverings, easy to clean, durable. Comes in wide range of colors and designs.

For any of these floorings, soften the appearance and reduce the clatter with an attractive area rug, which can be turned or removed for cleaning. As a gentle reminder that this rug is not to be used for wiping feet, keep a rush or a cocoa mat just outside the door. Indoor/outdoor carpeting may seem practical for use in the entrance area, but it, too, will soil at crucial traffic spots.

The entrance area is a perfect place to display small trinkets that are important to you, such as travel mementoes or special collections. In our house we have a small whatnot shelf which holds molded and sculptured mushrooms of wood, sea coral, crystal and marble. This collection starts many interesting conversations. Not only do our friends enjoy seeing them, but they take delight in helping our "garden" of mushrooms grow.

The key, however, to an effective entrance area is not the design scheme. It is *you*. You must be, as Paul wrote, *"given to hospitality"* (Rom. 12:13). Unless you show yourself warm and friendly, your guests will never feel welcome, no matter how inviting the wallpaper or warm the lighting.

Capturing the essence of the design in the Andersen home, the entrance area exudes a warm, yet tranquil, greeting. Floral paintings seem to come to life in the mirrored arrangement. The rug, another work of art, brings butterflies to complete the welcoming scene. ➤

CHAPTER FIVE

THE COZY CORNER

"Be still, and know that I am God."
Psalm 46:10

As a well-planned home is a sanctuary for the whole family, so each cozy corner is a sanctuary to its individual members. This place may be large or small, but it is important to have such a refuge where family members can relax alone or with others, a place for conversation, meditation and prayer. It is a familiar place one can be comfortable in, like a particular place at the dinner table.

I am amazed at how many people today put a great deal of effort into designing a comfortable living room, then neglect to avail themselves of the comfort of a cozy corner. Often, the head of the house would rather retire to his den without even knowing why he prefers it; but a snug, cozy corner would keep him with his family. Such a place should provide comfortable chair(s); an ottoman for the feet; ample table surface for coffee, books, and newspapers; a good reading lamp; possibly an afghan. That cozy corner can be even more inviting if it is well-lit and the rest of the room is in shadow. Admittedly, this is an ideal setting.

Should you have a very large living room with what seems like an awkward jog in it, consider this odd space as possibly a perfect place for your cozy corner, with seating for two or three. We have such a "jog" in our home with seating for four (see Photo, p. 14). When the weather does not permit using the deck, Annabelle will be in that corner early every morning, studying her Bible. Annabelle has the right idea; the cozy corner is a blessed sanctuary in which to seek God's peace for herself, her family and friends.

If your dining room is large enough to have a second, smaller table in it, you can have another cozy corner. But if you, like most of us, have a single dining table, why not use the place where you regularly sit as your dining room cozy corner? Where else could you find a more pleasant place for a cup-of-tea chat with friends?

Our family room has many cozy corners, providing a feeling of warmth for each of us. At one time or another, but with no regular pattern, we use each of them when the Andersen family gets together to read, to play, to pray (see Photo, p. 38).

It is convenient, but not necessary, to have many cozy corners. Our family also has lived in a confined apartment and a small house where we were content to arrange our cozy corner as best we could.

If space permits, the master bedroom's cozy corner should contain a small sofa and one or two comfortable lounge chairs—all upholstered in harmonious fabric and all of similar styles. If space limits you to having only one or two throw pillows on the bed, it is still important to have this special area.

A warm, inviting cozy corner in the master bedroom prevents children from feeling that the door to that room is a Berlin Wall. Instead, it can be a special place to be when they are not feeling well; when they need an extra portion of love and tenderness; when they need comforting after a trying day (children have those, too); when they need reassurance that they are forgiven for possible misdeeds of the day; or when they must learn the "statutes and judgments" which the Lord commanded, *"And thou shalt teach them diligently unto thy children, and shalt say of them when thou sittest in thine house..."* (Deut. 6:7).

Since a cozy corner can be available whether you live in a furnished room or in a mansion, why not set one up? From personal experience, I know that if you will use it as a personal sanctuary in which to seek and receive God's direction and blessing, as a place for quiet talks with other family members and as a place simply to be together, you will find an important source of spiritual strength.

I am amazed at how many people today put a great deal of effort into designing a comfortable living room, then neglect to avail themselves of the comfort of a cozy corner.

Cozy corner in the Andersen
family room—here, the glow in
the fireplace gives reason to the unusual works of art shown in the
accoutrements and in the firewood.

Cozy corner in the Andersen
master bedroom—a special place
for the parents to relax; for the
children when they are receiving
extra portions of love and tenderness. The afghan, knitted by
Georg Andersen's mother, gives
the area an extraordinary quality
of love.

CHAPTER SIX

THE LIVING ROOM

*"Be not forgetful to entertain strangers:
for thereby some have entertained angels unawares."*
Hebrews 13:2

Before redesigning your living room, you must clearly and carefully define what functions you want the room to perform. Decide how many guests you will normally welcome—eight is a congenial number. (But among friends, "any number can play.") Then provide comfortable seating for each member of your family and your guests. Above all, use the entire room as a *living* room—not as the musty parlors of bygone years reserved for very special guests and very special occasions.

Compare what you need with what you have; any room can pleasantly handle only a certain amount of furniture for a certain number of functions. You must accept size limitations of your room gracefully, without asking the impossible.

For instance, do you want or need a game area—checkers, chess, card games? An area for movie/slide projection? A display or collection area—books, porcelain plates, etc.?

Also, do you want a music area, with a stereo or piano? In our living room the piano issues an open invitation to our children to use the room freely. And we become more close-knit when we share our talents around the piano as a family or with our guests.

For your music center, you might buy a cabinet or an armoire ranging from five to seven feet tall and use it to store your television, records and stereo components. Cut out the back of any cabinet not designed especially for television so that the heat can escape. This will allow you to close the doors on your video equipment. However, I have no professional quarrel with leaving the television screen exposed.

A personal note here: Since television, "warts and all," is here to stay, I encourage you to plan some family viewing times. These can be opportunities for discussion, in a low-key, non-threatening setting, on issues of values and morals.

What about heirlooms? which I define as treasures of the heart. One of our treasures is the pie safe in our kitchen, which once belonged to Annabelle's grandparents (see Photo, p. 46). It still has protruding heads of nails that her grandfather drove into it to splice cracked pieces of wood. Never would I consider replacing those nails to achieve a smoother piece of carpentry. Another such treasure is a rocking chair which has been in Annabelle's family for many years (see Photo, p. 47).

We usually think of heirlooms as aged things, but this isn't always true. My mother crocheted afghans for each of our children, and we consider these "heirlooms." For Kirsten's, she used predominantly white yarn with a chevron pattern in blue. For Kristian's, a matching blue predominates and a matching white forms the chevron pattern (note afghan on chair in Photo, p. 39). Appropriately, Kirsten's afghan seems more feminine and and Kristian's more masculine. For her afghan, our teenaged daughter, Katrina, chose hot pink, lavender, and green. My mother has also crocheted a white tablecloth which we use over green felt on our table during the Christmas holidays.

The monetary value of these heirlooms is unimportant. But the intrinsic value? Priceless!

Keep the living room interesting but reserve "cleverness" for things that can be easily changed, such as colors and accessories. Anything "built in," of course, is difficult to change.

Should you have a green thumb, I encourage you to get as much of God's greenery into your living room as possible. Nothing more effectively gives life to a sparsely furnished room. If you, like my dear wife, Annabelle, have a "brown" thumb, I strongly urge that you experiment with plants which do not require much attention; or ask your local nurseryman for suggestions. Rarely have I heard of anyone having problems raising Swedish ivy or spider plants.

When your plants begin to flourish, overcome the natural tendency to let them continue their prolific growth. Paradoxical as it might seem, you must prune them. As Jesus said, "...*every branch that bears fruit, He prunes it, that it may bear more fruit*" (John 15:2, NASB).

Above all, use the entire room as a *living* room—not as the musty parlors of bygone years reserved for very special guests and very special occasions.

Photo on following page: Issuing an open invitation to use the Andersen living room freely, the piano also brings both beauty and musical delight to family and friends.

Furniture and its placement

The main considerations concerning furniture placement are *comfort* and *ease of conversation.*

Although high-backed sofas and chairs lend to the vertical feel of a room, they block vision unless they have see-through backs. Such high-backed furniture and certain pieces of large furniture will fit only along certain walls in your living room, depending on window/door occurrence. Place them there and work from that point.

Study the following sketches of furniture arrangements. Among them you will probably find one that will be close to that of your living room; make slight adjustments to get exactly what you desire.

An oversized sofa, eight feet long or more, can be made to look smaller by placing two lounge chairs or pull-up chairs to overlap each end of the sofa (at least to the inside of its arms). Then fill in the sofa with large, square pillows (19½" to 22"). The space between the pillows is thus reduced to about six feet. Since only two people can be conversationally comfortable on a sofa, the ideal size is between six and seven feet. Another way to "reduce" the size of a sofa is to cover it with a fabric the same color as walls and carpeting.

I've been asked quite often how to remedy a "too-small" sofa. There is no such thing. If it is very small, it is a settee, not a sofa, and should be used in a corner (on an angle), relegated to the entrance area or to a corner in the bedroom.

The main considerations concerning furniture placement are *comfort* and *ease of conversation.*

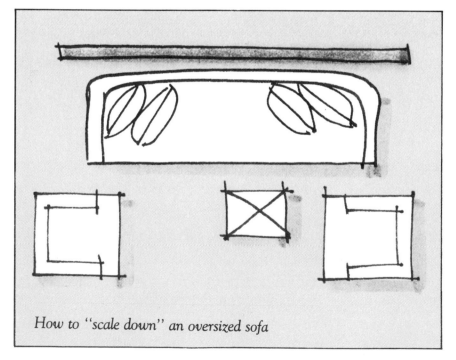

How to "scale down" an oversized sofa

If there is no fireplace, large cabinet, or 5' to 8' armoire (suggested as a possible furnishing for the music center), build a long, Parsons style table (see p. 63) or hang a 5' to 8' long ledge, 29" to 30" above the floor, as shown at the top of the drawing. Note the circular seating arrangement which allows for ease of conversation. Also note the extra pull-up stools under the long table. The sofa's size allows no room for end tables here, thus it is flanked by two floor lamps of equal height, giving much-needed illumination to this end of the room.

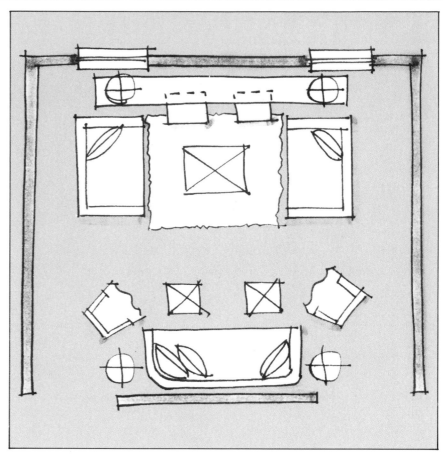

Photo on following page:
The pie safe in the Andersen kitchen belongs to Annabelle Andersen's grandparents. A treasure from another age, it not only brings charm and beauty to the room but it can be—and is—used regularly.

Photo on page 47:
This rocking chair is an Andersen heirloom. Given in love by Annabelle's parents, it is truly a treasure of the heart.

In a smaller room, such as the
one depicted here, upholstered
pieces can be placed as in the
drawing on page 45, but without open-arm chairs. Note the
lack of an area rug. Such a rug
in a small room will only split
the room up and accentuate its
small size.

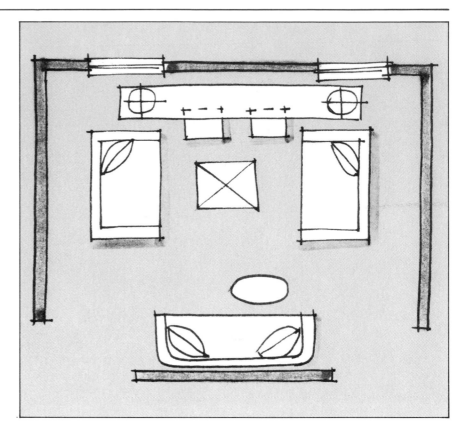

The antique, multi-colored, cotton
dhurrie rug reflects all of the colors
in the owner's mineral collection
displayed on the linen-lacquered
etageré.

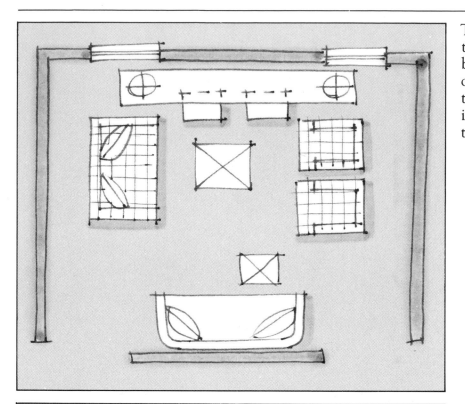

This is the same basic plan as in the drawings on pages 45 and 48, but here we use one loveseat opposite two lounge chairs. All three pieces should be covered in the identical fabric to give the area balance and symmetry.

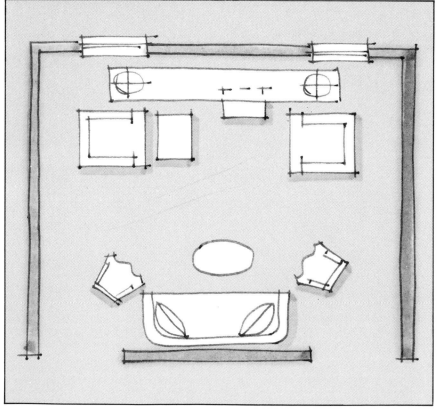

Here we use two lounge chairs. The stools of the three previous arrangements are replaced here with ottomans that serve as seating or as footrests. A pair of open-arm chairs is attractive and portable. If room size permits, a second pair in a different style may be added.

Try to have a table surface accessible to every seat in the room. Where two loveseats are sharing a coffee table, be certain that the table can be reached easily by the guests sitting on either loveseat. it may be wise to use two smaller tables (18" square), placing one in front of each loveseat and diagonally across from each other (as shown here).

You might try flanking a sofa with two tables—an 18" × 30" rectangular end table and a 30" round table. The round table could be skirted with felt, and then dramatized by the addition of taped designs along the bottom. Although end tables are normally 29" high, they should be either the exact height of the sofa arm or 2" higher or lower than the sofa arm.

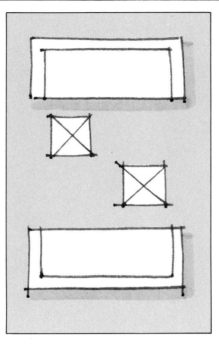

Try to have a table surface accessible to every seat in the room.

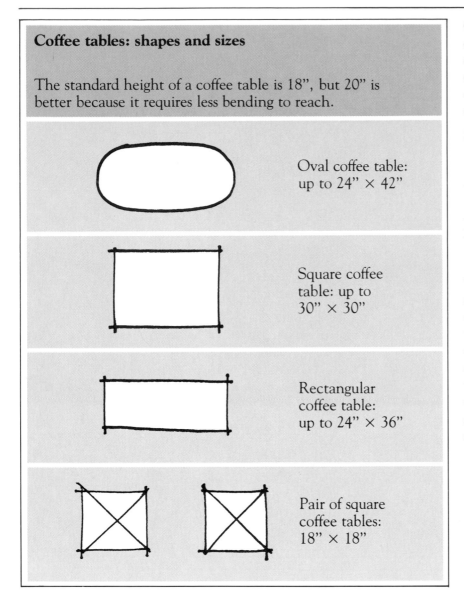

Coffee tables: shapes and sizes

The standard height of a coffee table is 18", but 20" is better because it requires less bending to reach.

Oval coffee table: up to 24" × 42"

Square coffee table: up to 30" × 30"

Rectangular coffee table: up to 24" × 36"

Pair of square coffee tables: 18" × 18"

Coffee tables may be constructed of wood and painted or stained, or covered with leather, fabric, or vinyl; they may be fashioned of glass, with brass or chrome; or they even may be mirrored.

Small, stacking bamboo tables (which often can be purchased in sets of three) next to, or between, a pair of chairs are attractive and practical. Such pieces would not be advisable for a period room.

Bamboo-style cane or rattan furniture also makes practical serving or storage pieces. Small chests can be used to brighten up an entrance area; larger chests provide beauty and storage in any room. And one or two classic, curved, Oriental chairs bring a touch of richness and warmth to a conversation area.

In the subtly sophisticated Andersen
living room, the dhurrie rug, an
outstanding work of art, is the
color palette not only for the room
but for the entire Andersen home.

Living room lighting

Ideally, there should be no ceiling (down) lighting in the living room except over game tables, and that should operate on a separate switch. In order to eliminate unattractive shadows, living room lighting should come predominantly from table or floor lamps (see Photo, p. 53).

While there are many other wonderful styles of lamps, basic vase and canister styles are the most suitable. Lamps fashioned from old boots, coffee percolators, or shiny teakettles are usually rather "hokey" and do not "wear well." Use such items as accessories, *not* lamps.

Table lamps and shades should not exceed 30" in height or they will overpower the room. Also, a greater height will give an unsightly view up into the shade to the bare light bulb. Lamps shorter than 30" are more desirable for reading because their bulbs will be closer to you. Tables on which lamps sit should never be lower than 24" or higher than 29".

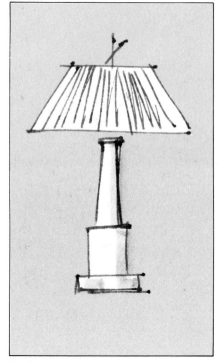

Column

Crystal   Metal
Lucite   Porcelain

Chinese Ginger Jar

Multi-colored porcelain
Solid-colored porcelain
Silvered glass

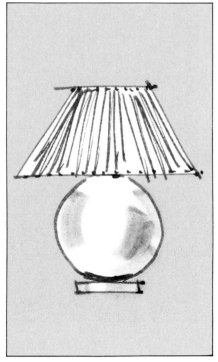

Ball

High polish metal
White plaster

There are not many attractive floor lamps on the market today. If you own an old one, put a new shade on it and keep it. There is no better reading lamp than a standard floor lamp that can throw a good light over your right or left shoulder.

The tent and pharmacy lamps, shown below, are the most popular floor lamps available today. Used in a contemporary setting, they are ideal; used in a period setting, they may add a delightfully contemporary note. In pairs they are charming but furnish only accent lighting; they can accept no stronger than a 60-watt bulb, so they are certainly not suitable for reading which requires 100 watts or more. (Most table lamps provide for three-way bulbs, which are 75-, 100-, 150-watt—or for a double swivel socket, which uses two 60-watt bulbs.)

Standard floor lamp
Metal
Clear glass rod

In order to eliminate unattractive shadows, living room lighting should come predominantly from table or floor lamps.

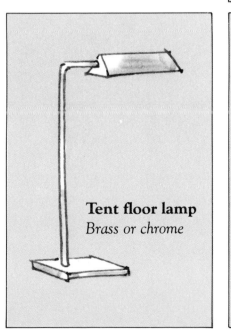

Tent floor lamp
Brass or chrome

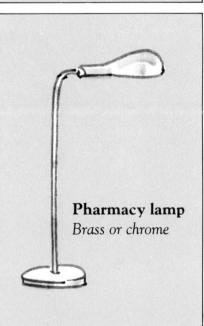

Pharmacy lamp
Brass or chrome

Below are some examples of typical lamp shade styles.

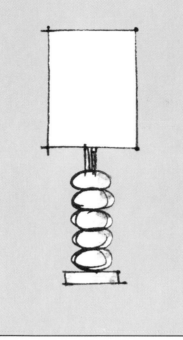

Extreme taper

Very small at top, broad at base; gives a "snappy" look to column lamps and some porcelain shapes.

Drum type

Used ideally in commercial situations—hotel lobbies, etc.; the style is almost always too severe to be flattering in a home.

Gentle taper

Easy on the eye; accentuates what is beneath it.

Most lamps currently on the market with tapered shades have been professionally scaled and will be quite attractive. (One brand you can always depend on for good professional scaling is Tyndale.)

Shades are available in many types of material. Personally, I prefer very simple shades without a lot of contrast in the color of the trimming, which is normally found at the top and the bottom of the shade. My favorite shade is pleated linen, available in most department stores across the country.

If you now own lamps where the height of the shades is excessive, you can buy new harps at any hardware store. These will allow you to alter the placement of the shade on its base.

Although it may take a bit of getting used to, a lamp shade should be strongly tapered. A good general size is 8" to 10" in diameter at the top, 16" to 18" at the bottom, and 12" to 16" on the slant.

To be sure you choose the right shade, indulge in some trial-and-error "window" shopping in the lamp-shade department. You may even want to take home the shade you select and try it on your lamp. In case you will need to return it to the store, handle it with special care and keep the cellophane wrapping intact. If you do keep the shade, tear that cellophane or plastic off in a hurry and enjoy the beauty of the lamp shade!

Note the pleasing proportion and shape of the pleated linen shade on the yellow porcelain ginger jar lamp. With a correctly proportioned shade, your eye more readily realizes the beauty of the lamp base.

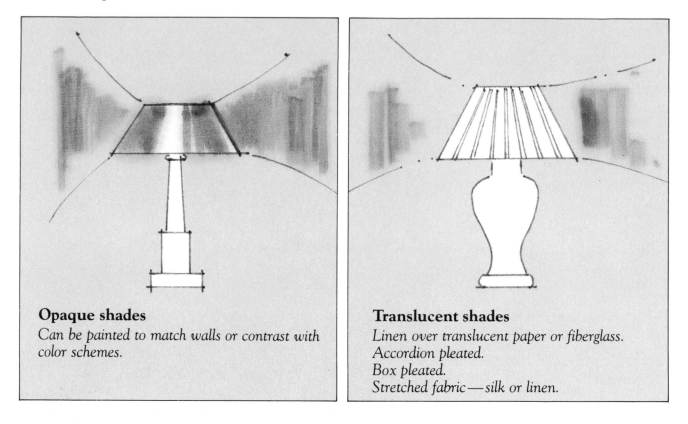

Opaque shades

Can be painted to match walls or contrast with color schemes.

Translucent shades

Linen over translucent paper or fiberglass.
Accordion pleated.
Box pleated.
Stretched fabric—silk or linen.

Thick, translucent shades give even, gentle, pleasant illumination to a room, and produce only faint shadow lines on the walls. Opaque shades of paper or painted metal, known as tôle, create very interesting and dramatic shadows that play against the wall. These shades will project a strong, inverted "U", or arc, of light from the bottom of the shade and a strong, dramatic configuration from the top.

Whether you use opaque or translucent shades is entirely a matter of preference. A room can easily handle both types of shades. Opaque shades are very practical on writing-table lamps, for they throw a strong light down onto the writing surface.

Special lighting

A light often installed in the ceiling of the living room, the "wall washer," is not a down light but a recessed fixture which aims a splash of light toward the wall. A track-mounted wall washer is also an option. Available at electrical supply stores, such fixtures are most effective when installed 24" to 30" from the wall and used to spotlight a painting or a stone or paneled wall. When planning the direction of the light, beware of reflective surfaces; the reflection will bring a harsh, distracting glare into the room. Mirrors, glass, and highly polished woods are the principal offenders.

When planning the direction of the light, beware of reflective surfaces; the reflection will bring a harsh, distracting glare into the room.

Always keep in mind that the interior design of your home is an expression of your personality and that of your family.

My favorite way of adding drama and interest when lighting a room is with the use of floor-can lamps. Usually 5" in diameter or 5" square by 10" high, they are "up" lights that use flood bulbs. Tuck one or more into the corners of the room and they will cast a dramatic light that hits the ceiling, bounces back down and filters through the room. When placed under large, indoor trees or plants, they trace the intricate designs of leaves in intriguing shadow patterns on the ceiling.

Shy away from sconce lighting in the living room. However, it is not uncommon to flank a fireplace with mounted hurricane lights. Admittedly, when used as lights instead of decorations, these do nothing to flatter the appearance of people in the living room. Much preferred over electrified sconces are hurricane lamps that hold candles. Don't be timid about lighting the candles when the occasion warrants.

Another intriguing way of bringing light into your living room involves a strip of series lighting in the upper portion of a glass-shelved, open cabinet. These lights are similar to old-fashioned, screw-in, Christmas-tree lights. Use four bulbs for every three feet of cabinet length.

A fireplace, even without a fire, offers another special way to bring light into the living room. Simply place two or three votive candles on the grate and light them. If the candles themselves can be placed out of sight behind, for instance, the bottom edge of the fireplace screen, the lights will give a mysterious flickering glow.

Some of the interior-design components mentioned in this chapter may be easily adapted for use in other rooms of your house. For instance, the design in most rooms can be improved with the proper use of greenery, appropriate lighting, and, in most cases, placement of furniture. Always keep in mind that the interior design of your home is an expression of your personality and that of your family. Therefore, don't let yourself be intimidated by the principles of good design. Master them, be creative and make them work for you.

In the Andersen dining room, the always practical Duncan Phyfe set blends with the floor and the corner tables, giving a beautiful contrast to the floral rug and curtains. ➤

CHAPTER SEVEN

THE DINING ROOM

*"Whether therefore ye eat, or drink, or whatsoever ye do,
do all to the glory of God."*

1 Corinthians 10:31

The dining room, or dining area, must offer comfort, convenience and a pleasant environment. The basic function of the room, meals, is quite clearly established, but it is important that you determine how many people will be seated for *most* occasions. Seating for eight often works out to be the most congenial, as well as practical. A dining room cluttered with unneeded chairs looks like a room where a corporate board of directors meets, not where friends will enjoy dining together.

There is nothing like dining with friends to establish rapport. As Samuel Pepys wrote, "Strange to see how a good dinner...reconciles everybody." In our home, as we thank God for our food, we always ask Him to bless and inspire our conversation. Many wonderful evenings have drawn to a close with all of us still at our dining table because of what Pope calls "the sweeter banquet of the mind."

Of course, you must determine the type of service. Will yours usually be a dinner where guests sit down and are served? Or will it be a dinner served family style? Or will it be the current popular method of serving dinner, especially to a larger group, the buffet style?

A small dining room can handle only one table gracefully. That table should be 36" to 42" wide. If you are serving eight people, the table should be about 7' long. Each person seated should have a minimum of 24" of "frontage" at the table, preferably more. The table's shape, be it oval, rectangular or round, is not as important as its capacity.

Quite often those who own large dining rooms have another "satellite" table, usually referred to as a breakfast table, that seats two to four people. It is quite convenient, especially at a buffet service. When two tables are used, the host sits at one and the hostess at the other.

A drop-leaf breakfast table should open to become a round table of 36" to 42" in diameter when the leaves are raised. One way to enlarge a small, nonextendable table is to place a piece of plywood, approximately 54" in diameter, on top of the table. Skirt it with an attractive cloth that hangs to the floor and you have a gala dining table. Or for more comfort in seating, the cloth need drop only 14".

Choosing a table

First, you might consider the Duncan Phyfe, a very handsome but rather common style. It is also practical; it has one or two pedestals which means there are no legs to get in the diners' way. By watching newspaper ads, yard sales and auctions, you can frequently buy this type of table for a fraction of its original cost. In fact, a few years ago at a moving sale, we paid only $40 for our attractive Duncan Phyfe dining set with six, rush-bottom, ladder-back chairs. It had been well cared for by the previous owner and required no restoration (see Photo, p. 61).

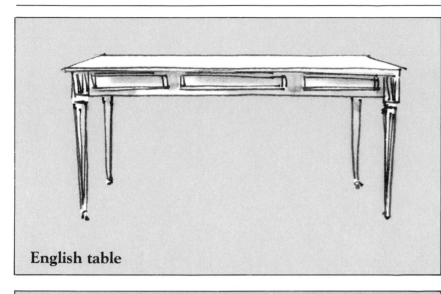

English table

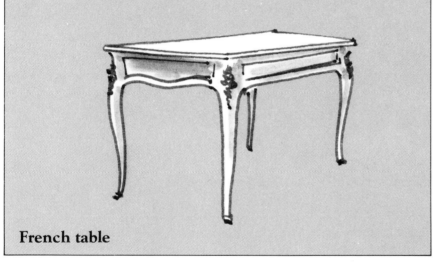

French table

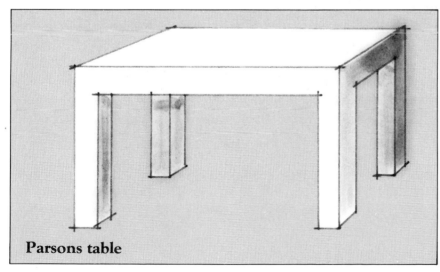

Parsons table

The basic, four-legged dining table is also practical. It can be found in a number of styles: Period French, English, or today's very popular and versatile Parsons style.

The Parsons table, which gets its name from the Parsons School of Design in New York, can be any size and can be used as a dining table, end table or coffee table. If made of wood, it can be varnished, painted or even fabric-covered. It is also available in marble. It is especially effective when covered in Formica, which is heat and scratch resistant and available in a wide range of vibrant colors. Many lumber yards are equipped to build Parsons tables at a nominal cost.

Clear, glass-topped dining tables have enjoyed great popularity. They are beautiful but demanding, losing their grace when placed on an uninteresting floor. Many people dining at a glass-topped table, without a cloth, feel uncomfortable looking down at someone else's knees. The glass top shows every fingerprint and every wet-glass ring. Accordingly, the hosts are tempted to bring out the Windex for a clean-up job between courses. Still, there is no denying that this is a very pleasant table when placed on a beautifully patterned rug, be it floral or geometric.

Such tables are most effective in a small room where a light appearance helps to make the room look larger. Glass-topped tables, of course, do not extend.

A floral centerpiece low enough to
see over on the dining room table.

Because the walls were paneled,
we had no choice but to wallpaper
the ceiling and soffit in order to
get much-needed pattern and color
into our all-white kitchen. ➤

Dining room chairs

It is not necessary to buy matched dining room chairs. I prefer four to six side chairs of one style (see Drawing, p. 67), perhaps all wood, and possibly two fully upholstered wing chairs—or two open-arm chairs of even another style or finish to serve as host and hostess chairs. This diversity gives the dining room personality and character.

The illustrations on page 67 are pure period design and, as such, are very compatible when mixed. For instance, two Chip-pendale bamboo, open-arm chairs as host and hostess chairs work well with four Queen Anne side chairs. All of these chairs come in arm- or side-chair versions. When space permits, I prefer that each guest at the table have an arm chair. Since the luxury of a full 36" per place setting is out of reach for most people's budgets, today's quarters usually allow only the standard 24" per place setting, which requires side chairs.

Wing chair

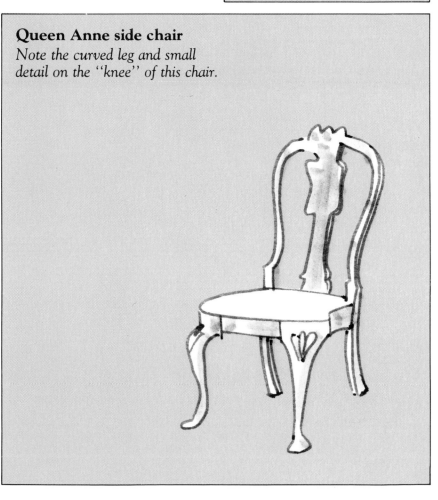

Queen Anne side chair
Note the curved leg and small detail on the "knee" of this chair.

Chippendale chair

This has a "ball and claw" foot.

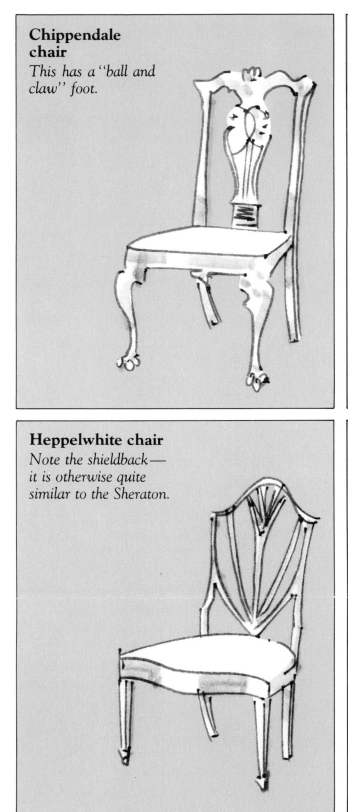

Sheraton chair

Note the straight top and elaborate nailhead detailing on the side of the chair.

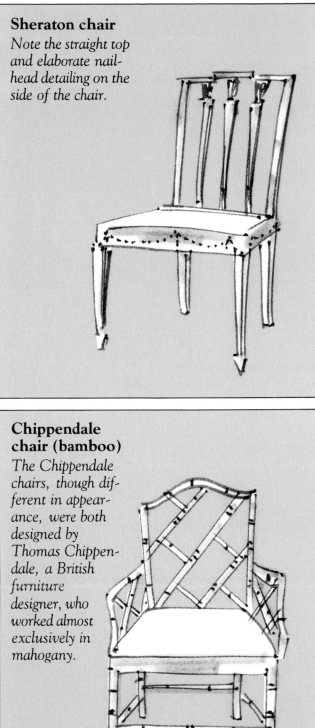

Heppelwhite chair

Note the shieldback— it is otherwise quite similar to the Sheraton.

Chippendale chair (bamboo)

The Chippendale chairs, though different in appearance, were both designed by Thomas Chippendale, a British furniture designer, who worked almost exclusively in mahogany.

Serving space

Provide as large a serving space as possible, preferably 16" to 18" deep by 5'6" long. This can be a serving counter mounted on the wall, 32" above the floor. Obviously, a buffet, in which silver, china, and crystal can be stored is more practical, but only in a large dining room. If the room is small, a serving table or cart without drawers (which the diner can see under) gives a much-needed feeling of space.

To beautify what could have been unsightly beams in the Andersen family room, the old, traditional American art of stenciling was used. For a personal touch, the children's names and birth dates were added. ➤

Dining room lighting

A chandelier in the dining room brings a pleasant, undulating sparkle to the table. It should be connected to a rheostat—such a tiny investment allows you to alter the mood of the room very easily; this permits dining in visual comfort but avoids harsh glare. This practice is also economical; a dimmer switch set to lower the output of the bulb to 60 percent of capacity will cut the energy cost by as much as 22 percent. This also will lengthen the life of the bulb. A chandelier should be installed 29" above the tabletop (from the top of the table to the bottom of the chandelier), or 58" above the finished floor. If possible, it should be centered over the table.

In my opinion, lack of overhead lighting in the dining room is no casualty. Very effective lighting comes from two pairs of sconces if each pair is installed on a wall opposite from the others. To give the most flattering light, they should all be controlled by the previously mentioned dimmer switch and should be 5'6" off the floor. Light coming from greater heights casts harsh shadows on people's faces and can be very unbecoming to women.

Although candlelight is expensive, messy and sometimes hot, it is the ideal dining room light, so you should try to emulate its effect. A very lovely form of light for dining is one in which candles are used in an unwired chandelier with bobeches (glass discs that hold candle drippings); the flickering, glowing light of the candles is supplemented by the very dim light of electric sconces on the wall.

Keep in mind that the lower the light intensity, the more pleasant and relaxed the entire space will appear. No one enjoys utter darkness, so do not allow the lighting to be so dim that people can't see what they are eating, much less enjoy the beauty of your table setting or the centerpiece you have arranged on the table. Show special thoughtfulness for older guests and others with poor vision by adjusting the light to a brighter level than usual.

Again, I suggest that you tuck floor-can lights under plants and greenery in the room. These lights in the corners of the dining room will dispel any suspicion of encroaching gloom.

In the dining room, wall washers should not be used to illuminate paintings. Here, picture-mounted lights are warmer because they use soft, low-wattage bulbs.

I would suggest, for those of you who do not have a separate room, that you define a distinct dining area by the use of tall plants or perhaps wallpapered screens.

CHAPTER EIGHT

THE FAMILY ROOM

"A happy family is but an earlier heaven."
John Bowring

Keep your family room just that—a room that makes every member of the family feel it is *his/her* room, where each is free to relax, enjoy favorite activities and friends.

Our family room has ample storage behind doors for toys, games and crafts. Especially important to Kirsten and to Kristian is the 2" lip on one shelf that prevents bats, balls and dolls from rolling off. Other shelves hold needlework for Annabelle and books for Katrina. We first considered it an unfortunate sacrifice to give up floor space for these cabinets, but we have never regretted it. What is that motto? "A place for everything, and everything in its place...."

There is ample room for Kirsten to set up her gymnast equipment and practice gymnastics, or for Kristian to work on his 4' × 5' electric train. Other members of the family either act as spectators or engage themselves in other pursuits.

Our family room is the largest room in our house. The previous owner, who had made working with youth groups a part of his life and ministry, built this room to accommodate about 65 young people from his church. We therefore can entertain a large number of people in the room. By design, we have a compact Pullman kitchen behind doors for preparing snacks (Kristian also uses the area to play with his chemistry set). (Named for the ones used on Pullman railroad coaches, kitchen units of this type are still manufactured by the Dwyer Company.)

Also by design, we have a second-floor deck that can hold as many as 100 people. Our outdoor furniture is white-painted wrought iron. However, high-gloss enameled wood or metal, heavily varnished wood or stained redwood would be just as satisfactory. Rattan and wicker pieces of furniture are attractive, but they must be taken in each night and during bad weather.

As I sit on our sun deck, I am grateful to the poet who so eloquently wrote:

"Live not without thy God;
However low or high
In every home should be
A window in the sky."

God cannot be contained within the walls of a furnished room or a mansion, so I thank Him for our "window in the sky."

Since Annabelle and I also work with youth groups from our church, we have dedicated the house to the Lord and carry on a ministry similar to that of the former owner. Frequently on Sunday evenings after church, or on Friday evenings after an athletic event, 25 to 50 high school and college students can be found at our house.

On a typical Sunday evening, our young guests come charging in after church. As though someone had given an order to disperse, they scatter throughout the house. To their great delight, there are no instructions—no formal program.

A huddle forms around the piano. Young voices join in gospel songs, moving from one song to the next so rapidly that we wonder how each voice follows the changes. A guitarist is in the huddle somewhere—we hear the instrument but we cannot see who is touching the strings. Psalm 66:1,2 is being fulfilled: *"Make a joyful noise unto God, all ye lands: sing forth the honour of his name: make his praise glorious."*

The party soon moves downstairs to the family room for pizza, crackers, cheese, chips, dips and soft drinks. In a matter of minutes, the snack area is clean and our young guests are sitting on the floor, on sofas and on chairs (both the seats and the arms). It seems that everybody's talking and nobody's listening, but they *are* communicating. Laughter in one cozy corner singles out a young man desperately drawing domino after domino from the "lumber yard" because he cannot add to the domino maze on the carpet. On the other side of the room, our stuffed donkey flies like a wingless Pegasus from one pair of hands to another.

The joy-filled evening eventually comes to a close as the piano softly sends out a musical benediction....

It is for evenings such as this that the floor covering in the family room should combine practicality (ease of maintenance) and beauty. Our family room has green-plaid indoor/outdoor carpeting; but linoleum, or wood with a polyurethane finish would be just as practical.

Sofa fabric for the family room should be soft and pleasant to touch; and where possible, use easy-to-maintain natural fibers. Avoid plastic and naugahyde; though they wipe clean easily, they are not very inviting.

A family room requires a wide variety of lighting. Over game tables, it is wise to use down lighting installed *in* the ceiling, as opposed to surface-mounted lights. In other areas of the room, down lighting only gives a feeling of starkness, even harshness. I prefer table lamps and floor lamps. The family room should be equipped for bright illumination for playing games, etc., and also have soft, low lighting for the later hours when perhaps Mom and Dad are there alone. A complete grid of down lighting dispersed all over the ceiling is unattractive and definitely not intimate.

Depending upon the size of the room and its predetermined functions, a desk for answering correspondence, bookkeeping, and bill-paying would be an interesting and efficient addition to the family room. It can be either a tabletop or a rolltop desk. The former, when cleared, can be used as a game table; the latter would provide the added convenience of being able to literally drop the lid on any unfinished work until a later time. A desk can be even a brightly lacquered Parsons table, or a pair of sawhorses—or any other available base—with a wood or a glass top.

A family room is a great convenience. However, if you do not have a family room, per se, adjust your sights and design your living room to serve as both.

The Andersen sun deck, their "window in the sky," not only gives joy to the family and friends but is a necessary companion to the large family room. For, as a part of their Christian ministry, the Andersens often invite as many as 65 young people from their church into their home.

In a corner of the Andersen family room, a game table with down lighting (one of very few places that such lighting should be used). ➤

CHAPTER NINE

THE MASTER BEDROOM

"My soul shall be satisfied with marrow and fatness; and my mouth shall praise thee with joyful lips: when I remember thee upon my bed, and meditate on thee in the night watches."

Psalm 63:5-6

As the principal sanctuary of the home, the master bedroom should be gentle, warm, intimate, and as clutter-free as possible; and it should be conducive to relaxation. It is a special place where husband and wife share joy and love, a place where they truly comprehend the Swedish saying that "shared joy is double joy; shared sorrow is half-sorrow."

It is important that husband and wife arrange their priorities in such a way that they have scheduled free time together — time to chat, to pray, and to use the special way God planned for them to say to each other, "I love you." If they keep this free-time date throughout their married life, they will surely maintain that special closeness and love that makes a strong, delightful marriage.

My many years as an interior designer have taught me that if a client likes the organization of the master bedroom, everything else in the house seems to fall into its proper place. Since many of my clients work long hours, quite frequently this is the only room they really see except on weekends. Consequently, I encourage them to begin their design work there.

Because the bed is the central object in this room, choose yours carefully. You will spend a third of your life in it! The size of the bed, in proportion to the size of the room, may dictate where the bed should go. If possible, it should not be visible through the door; there will be times, even in the best-run home, when the bed will not be made — an unmade bed is not very pleasant to look at.

Another major consideration for a bedroom is storage space. There should be ample space for his/her clothes and personal belongings. Instead of a dresser with drawers, which are not really necessary, I prefer built-in adjustable shelves from floor to ceiling, enclosed by louvered doors (see Photo, p. 78). These shelves will hold as much as a large dresser and will require only half as much floor space. An etagere (open-shelved cabinet) is equally adaptable for storage, and it is less expensive than built-in shelves.

Sets of matching furniture are too dull and predictable for the home, especially for the master bedroom. Perhaps one bedside table should be round and skirted; the other could have a shallow drawer for pencils, note pads and tissue. One table could be made of wicker; the other of brass, mahogany, or pine.

The color of a bedroom should be soft and pleasant, and mutually agreed upon by husband and wife. Because rest is a major reason for this room, I recommend relaxing colors. We have chosen blue for ours (see Photo, pp. 76-77).

The floor covering of the bedroom should also look and feel soft. This is why I favor wall-to-wall carpeting.

Lighting in the master bedroom

With the exception of an excellent reading light in the cozy corner (either a table or a floor lamp), bedroom lighting should be soft and minimal. My favorite lighting for reading in bed is shown below (also see Photo, p. 79).

This lamp will extend to the bed. It releases space on the bedside table for books, magazines, clock radio, or whatever is needed. It provides adequate light for reading and also illuminates the room with a soft glow.

Window treatment

A good window treatment for the master bedroom could begin with white-eyelet, tieback curtains. Panels of overcurtains in printed fabric can hang at either side of the eyelets. These do not draw shut, but do bring extra color into the bedroom.

Since our house is nestled in the woods and our master bedroom is on the second floor, we do not concern ourselves with the need for privacy. In another location we would probably need roller shades on the windows.

An inexpensive way to obtain print fabric is to purchase bed sheets. Our own bedroom incorporates a very popular sheet design that I helped to develop. Top designers are paid well for these designs, and there is a wide selection from which to choose. Yet, the sheets are available throughout the country at a cost lower than the per-yard retail price of such fabric.

Since the husband-wife relationship is the key to a happy family, and if proper interior design can enhance a person's relationship with God, himself and others (spouse included), then the master bedroom deserves primary attention as you redesign your home. If God's love, peace and order can permeate this room, the entire house will be influenced by their fragrance.

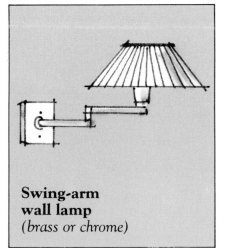

**Swing-arm
wall lamp**
(brass or chrome)

*Photo on following page:
As in the Andersen master bedroom, the husband and wife should select a mutually acceptable, soft and pleasant color scheme. Also, wall-to-wall carpeting adds a certain softness to the well-dressed bedroom.*

The Andersen bedside table with concealed drawer and shelf storage. Note the swing-arm wall lamps which release space on the floor or table surfaces for books, magazines, a clock radio, or whatever is needed.

The Andersen master bedroom showing storage shelves which hold as much as a large dresser and require only half the floor space.

CHAPTER TEN

BEFORE YOU GO SHOPPING

"Not what we have, but what we use;
Not what we see, but what we choose—
These are the things that mar or bless
The sum of human happiness."

Clarence Urmy

Before you begin to invest in furniture, wall coverings, or accessories, make certain that you now understand the basic steps needed to properly design your home's interior. Carefully read through the following summary; then you will be ready to follow the shopping instructions.

1. Your home, like your body, should be used to glorify God.

2. Your home cannot be an effective expression of God's character unless your life is.

3. Good interior design does contribute to contentment and joy. However, be content with what you have while you work to achieve your design goals.

4. From your favorite home magazine(s), cut out photos of rooms that you like at first glance. Do *not* study them. Store them in a folder until you have forty or fifty.

5. Honestly analyze your collection of photos. Ask, "What at-a-glance features persuaded me to retain each picture? Do certain colors recur? What other factors keep recurring?"

6. In answer to your questions, make notes about the pictures. Regroup them according to the patterns that have developed (you may want to study the case history in Appendix A). You *are* beginning to know what you really like.

7. Do not rush the analytical phase; you will undoubtedly want to lay the pictures aside at times in order to get a fresh perspective later.

8. To determine exactly what you already have, take a room-by-room inventory of your furniture, accessories, and works of art, including their dimensions.

The landing on our stairway is a contrast between an impressionistic painting and a rustic, Norwegian-decorated churn.

9. Because you cannot make use of your room inventories until the picture-collecting and analytical phases are completed, use the intervals to acquire a good, working knowledge of the basic principles of design (Chap. Three); learn the use of color, paneling, window treatment, lighting, wall coverings and floor coverings.

10. Construct a swatchboard as described and illustrated in Chapter Three.

11. Plan carefully the entrance area (Chap. Four) for your home. It should be especially charming and also in complete agreement with the design and atmosphere in the rest of your house.

12. The Cozy Corner (Chap. Five), large or small, is a place to relax, dream, chat, or, more important, to commune with God. If space permits, cozy corners should be found in the living room, dining room, family room and master bedroom.

13. Clearly define the functions you want the living room (Chap. Six) to perform. Game area? Projection area? Display or collection area? Make your design fit these functions.

14. Get as much of God's greenery into your rooms as possible. Water, feed and prune plants to enhance growth.

15. Study the drawings, pages 44-51, for living-room furniture arrangements; these will readily, or with slight changes, adapt to almost any room. Ideally, there should be no ceiling (down) lighting in the living room except over game tables. Lighting should come predominantly from table or floor lamps. Review the methods of special living room lighting (pp. 54-60).

16. As you plan your dining room, first determine the number of guests and usual manner of serving you expect to have. Also, decide on a table and chairs (see pp. 63-67). Dining room lighting is explained on page 68. If you have a dining *area* instead of a specific room, the same principles apply. But do set the area off with large plants or attractive screens.

17. The family room (Chap. Eight) should make every member of the family feel that it is his/her room. It should contain storage space for games, crafts, books and magazines. The floor covering should combine beauty with ease of maintenance. Again, install no down lighting except over game tables.

18. As the principal sanctuary of the home, the master bedroom (Chap. Nine) should be gentle, warm, intimate, and as clutter-free as possible. Husband and wife should regularly schedule free time together. This room's color should be soft and pleasant, and mutually agreed upon by husband and wife. Wall-to-wall carpeting brings softness to the room. Matching furniture is too dull and predictable. Except for reading lamps, lighting should be soft and minimal. Use window treatment only as required for privacy.

19. Begin to look around carefully in department stores, specialty shops, secondhand stores, discount stores and junk shops for "best buys."

20. Remember that making God the Head of your home is the most important step in your interior-design journey.

Shopping instructions

First, arm yourself with a budget, a notebook, and your swatch-board. You are now ready to go on a fact-finding, window-shopping tour. Get prices on everything you need for your finished room: furniture, fabrics, wall coverings, floor coverings, lamps and other accessories. Back at home, organize your facts. At this time, study Appendix B—"Budget-Cutting Ideas."

Now you may go shopping to begin your buying.

It is probably best to shop for one room at a time, but during each trip, be alert for purchases for other rooms. Which room you shop for first depends upon your priorities. I, of course, prefer to start with the master bedroom.

When shopping for fabric, get information on its wearability and maintenance requirements. It is often smart to buy more fabric for throw pillows than you need, so that you can re-cover them as they wear out. However, don't become upset by that "lived-in" look that will inevitably appear. Upkeep and replacement are a part of living.

As you prepare to purchase furnishings, you will need to consider what you *like* against what you need. Do you truly like the things you are buying? If so, you are not apt to get tired of them. Do you actually *need*, or do you simply *want*, that expensive sofa? Remember that if the less-expensive sofa is adequate, you can splurge on good-quality throw pillows and be rewarded with a more beautifully furnished effect in your room. On the other hand, do not compromise too quickly on things you really want.

Beware of buying furniture where seating is so low it is difficult to get in or out of. This problem is especially common with some contemporary pieces.

These days there is almost no restriction on mixing periods of furniture. However, there should be 75 to 85 percent of one type so as to establish whether the room is predominantly period or contemporary. Beware of trends; they are "planned obsolescence."

Be sure your interior design plan does not "overwork" any room. Each room can pleasantly handle only a certain amount of furniture for a certain number of functions.

Whatever you have and wherever you are, first of all, consider what you have and thank God for it. Then sit back and ask, "How closely am I adhering to my design plans? Have I established, and am I acting on, my priorities (i.e., correct the oversized lamp **shades**; make the curtains compatible with the wall color; wait on the new sofa since I can make the oversized one 'comfortable looking'— Drawing, p. 44)?" Commit yourself to fulfilling these plans which you formulated through careful study and thought. Don't be sidetracked by a sudden whim.

CHAPTER ELEVEN

ACCESSORIES

"The ornaments of a house are the friends who frequent it."
Ralph Waldo Emerson

The "knick-knacks," collections, art objects, paintings and, yes, even the books displayed give our homes personality. Even more than our choice of furniture styles, these room decorations make a personal statement to family and friends. Your most treasured accessories may not necessarily have great monetary value—family keepsakes, mementos of your travels, a child's first attempts at drawing or crafts often are familiar and well-loved elements in a particular room.

Of course, a child's piece of art may more appropriately fit in a family room or game room than in a rather formal dining room; but I will give you some guidelines for collecting and displaying your family's cherished memorabilia.

Without accessories, an otherwise attractively designed room can look unfinished and cold. Although the word "accessories" implies that they are not essential in themselves, you might call them the "supporting cast" of interior design.

Earlier in this book, I have discussed the importance of accessories, then shown their use through photographs and sketches. Wall decorations, throw pillows, plants and flowers, tables, lamps, sconces, candles and area rugs—all have been considered, some in detail.

How do you start selecting pieces that add that finishing touch to any room? That must be an individual decision. For instance, you might study the accessories in the pictures you have collected (Chap. Two), then purchase similar ones. However, you probably already have more accessories than you think. So, inventory the accessories you already possess—the ones you've bought just because you liked them and the ones friends have given you. You may discover you own a great surplus of accessories, many of which are either being stored in the basement or are not being displayed to their greatest advantage.

Unfortunately, some people believe they must spend a great deal of money on and a great deal of time searching for accessories. Not only do these people waste money and time that could be spent more wisely, but in far too many cases, they delay the full use of a room or two. "Perfection" is a fine thing to strive for, but in the meantime, be bold enough to improvise.

In my family's case, our house had to be "child-proof" for several years. Until all our babies had outgrown the "wrecking ball" stage, important (or should I say, expensive?) accessories had to settle for obscure places or be stored. In their stead, rugged, natural items such as pieces of sea coral or mineral (geodes, for instance) assumed places of importance on our coffee table and lamp tables. Beyond their aesthetic value, these items also were teaching tools. They exposed our children to, and gave us a chance to discuss, the varied facets of God's creation.

As another "child-proof" measure, we sometimes have placed a collection of hand-made, wooden toys on our family-room table (see Photo, p. 86). We then enjoy watching the creativity, and, even more, the delight of youngsters, young and old, as they play with these toys.

Centerpieces

Centerpieces are always a delightful accessory. We have often put three small, potted plants of the same type on a wicker tray to serve as the focal point of our dining table or coffee table. When we need flowers for our own pleasure or for a dinner party, we buy from a nursery eight to twelve tiny pots of blooming plants, which are usually quite inexpensive.

Poked into a wicker basket, along with moss and English ivy cut from our garden, these make a spring-like arrangement with much more personality than anything available at the florist's. And we do it for less than a fourth of the cost.

Another very colorful centerpiece we use on our dining table is a similar arrangement of plantings in a large wicker basket and in two miniature, flanking baskets. Fortunately, Annabelle has a collection of these baskets in all sizes. Occa-

sionally, we take porcelain birds from their perches in our living room cabinet and place them between the baskets. We enjoy watching our guests' delighted surprise as they discover our "fine feathered friends" nesting in table greenery.

Remember, a floral centerpiece for the dining table must be low enough to see over (see Photo), lacy enough to see through, or high enough to see under (such as nosegays wired to candelabra).

One of the most fascinating dining centerpieces I've ever seen was a fresh piece of sod fitted onto a large oval platter, studded with crocus and cuttings of hyacinth and other small blooms. The artist had reproduced a lush, flowering spring lawn in miniature. Should you be interested in duplicating this, a piece of sod can be purchased quite inexpensively at the local nursery along with a handful of cut flowers. I prefer such simple, natural dining centerpieces over the "store-bought" variety. And having "done it myself" always gives a special sense of satisfaction. So go ahead and try it! You don't have to be an artist to be creative.

Collections

At the moment, our most ambitious accessories are my personal collection of camels, most of which were gifts (see Photo, p. 30). As though they were assembled for a camel convocation, they stand or crouch on an end table. They have come in pewter, silver, gold plate, olive wood, stone, or twigs—this one carved for me by my son, Kristian. One large brass camel sits alone on a nearby coffee table (see Photo, p. 89).

Though far outnumbered by Job's reputed 4,000 camels, my camels have sparked many interesting conversations by their stately presence.

Books

I love books but I don't consider them accessories as such. They are far too important for that categorization. In my judgment, they belong in a bookcase or on shelves, with no sculptures, plants or paintings scattered among them. Regardless of size, each book's spine should stand flush with the edge of the shelf. If space remains for accessories on the shelves, these should be placed on separate shelves and should be grouped together by color, by material, or by type; that is, vases with vases, porcelains with porcelains, brass candlesticks with brass candlesticks, etc. But don't worry if there is room only for books. If you love reading as much as I do, a shelf filled with books will be an expression of your personality.

Still life

The landing on our stairway displays a beautiful impressionistic painting and a rustic churn, decorated with colorful, Norwegian rosemaling. The two create a pleasant contrast. The churn has its own individual charm and beauty, and when filled with fresh, blossoming tree branches reaching to the second story, the trip up or down a "living" stairwell is a very enjoyable experience (see Photo, p. 80). The churn, like all other well-placed accessories, expresses to all who enter the Norwegian word for "Welcome" —"*Velkommen.*"

So look over your picture collection again, noting specifically the accessories and arrangements which appeal to you. Then you are ready to duplicate or expand on these ideas in your own home.

"*Child-proof*" *accessories, a collection of handmade, mobile toys on the family room table.*

CHAPTER TWELVE

HOSPITALITY

*"...like a fashionable host
That slightly shakes his parting guest by the hand,
And with his arms outstretch'd, as he would fly,
Grasps in the comer: welcome ever smiles,
And farewell goes out sighing."*

William Shakespeare,
Troilus and Cressida

Christian hospitality begins when you invite God to become the permanent Head of your home. True hospitality preempts pride. It does not try to impress people but to serve them. It says, "This house is a gift of God; to glorify Him, I want to share it and all that I have with others."

In *Open Heart—Open Home*, Karen Burton Mains says that it doesn't matter if your rooms are small because God will find a way to expand the walls or compress the people. And true hospitality will flourish only when you open your home to others. So don't wait until you have new carpeting, or a better sofa or more chairs. With that attitude, there will always be one or two things you will "need" before you can invite friends, old or new.

Unavoidable pressures of today's living have required us to emphasize relaxed relationships. So make your guests feel at home—free to remove their coats, loosen their ties and kick off their shoes; to put their feet on the coffee table, or sit on the floor; or, if they arrive early, to help you set the table or toss the salad.

Far too often we procrastinate in this matter of showing Christian hospitality. I personally know people who live in relative luxury, but are not happy with their home. These people want to share what they have, but they are insecure and do not know how. They want to open their home to others but are fearful that "Our rug doesn't match the curtains"..."We need a special end table"..."The painting over the fireplace isn't quite right...."

Why don't these people begin to buy the things they "need"? They are insecure in making selections; they're never sure what they really do want. Many days, months, and years slip by, taking with them irrecoverable joys and pleasures these people might have known by sharing themselves and their homes with others.

Don't forget, however, that the coin of sharing has a reverse side. There are people who refuse invitations because "I would be out of place in a home like that"..."I can't afford to reciprocate in kind"..."I don't have," or, "I can't afford the proper clothes...."

With rare exceptions, a pleasant reception and true hospitality have greeted those who have boldly crossed the self-imposed barrier from either side.

We have small chairs tucked under a coffee table, an affirmation to our children and to our guests' children that they belong. The sense of acceptance is extremely important as a child enters the turbulent years of adolescence and young adulthood. Such small details can make the critical difference.

What, then, is true hospitality? Simply this: *"Thou shalt love thy neighbor as thyself"* (Mark 12:31b). In *Family Living in the Bible*, Edith Deen comments, "A golden thread running through the stories of the household of faith is the theme of hospitality. In New Testament times, this virtue was practiced, partly because it was an ancient custom, but, more significantly, because it was an expression of love for Jesus." We can do no less. I encourage you to begin this week!

It never occurred to Estelle to hesitate. She lived at a "swanky" address in Beverly Hills, but she joined a group of middle-income ladies who met Thursday afternoons for Bible study in their very modest homes in Los Angeles.

Estelle, in her mid-forties, was attractive, well groomed and always happy in the Lord. The ladies could not help loving her, but some of them stood in awe of her because of her fashionable address. And they could not understand why she would drive so far to join their group. Surely there were Bible study groups closer to her home.

At her third meeting, Estelle invited the ladies to meet at her home. They excused themselves with, "Too far." But Estelle prevailed and they accepted her invitation.

All were surprised and a bit humbled when she welcomed them to an unpretentious, sparsely furnished apartment over a garage behind a Beverly Hills mansion. Estelle thanked the ladies for coming and told them how delighted she had been to find a Bible study group that met on Thursday afternoons—the maid's day off!

For the Christian, hospitality is not a choice, it is a command: *"Be not forgetful to entertain strangers..."* (Heb. 13:2). And it should not be confined to guests. Rather, genuine hospitality should be so normal that each member of the family enjoys returning home from work, school, or play.

Children should be included in parties with family or friends as much as is possible within their schedules. As an adult, you probably remember and mentally reexperience the thrill of attending a "grown-up" party. Gradually, you learned to participate and thereby avoid embarrassment, such as young boys used to feel years ago when they wore their first pair of long pants.

Small chairs tucked under a coffee table, as in the Andersen living room, make small guests feel welcome.

CHAPTER THIRTEEN
STEWARDSHIP

"We are Goddes stewardes all, noughte of our owne we bare."

Thomas Chatterton

The word "steward" is derived from two English words, which together mean pigpen guard. The New Testament Greek word for stewardship meant "administration" or "economy"; it connoted a position of honor and dignity. "Stewardship" is now being pushed from our modern vocabulary because it is linked with rather negative and unpopular practices: budgets, collections, donations, etc.

A Christian steward has the perfect example in Jesus Christ who committed His entire life on earth to God. Thus, stewardship should not be based on "keeping up with the Joneses," but on keeping up with *Jesus.* A good steward knows that God decides what is best for him. If he owns a Victorian mansion and other luxuries, he will not be proud. If he rents a furnished room, he will not be ashamed. If he has only one talent or if he has many, they are gifts from God and he uses them to glorify the Lord.

The *"certain rich man"* (Luke 12:16-20) was not condemned for his riches, nor was the man who received only one talent (Matt. 25:15) condemned for his lack. Both were condemned for their improper stewardship of the Lord's gifts. So, when Paul said that the *"love of money is the root of all evil"* (1 Tim. 6:10), he laid the responsibility exactly where it belongs—on the *possessor,* not on the possessions.

The task of stewardship is one of spiritual challenge—one day we must give an account of the way we have managed God's gifts. And probably no matter challenges us more severely than does the disposition of our surplus. But when we prayerfully seek to serve Him, He gives incredible strength of character and ability to share.

Our giving testifies to our dependence on God. We must replace "mine, mine, mine" with "His, His, His," because He not only gives us what we have, He owns it. We are merely the managers of God's gifts. Today this can involve repairing what we have; not refusing offers of gifts from others; checking for bargains in newspaper advertisements, at yard sales, thrift shops, etc. We should do everything to increase the resources we can share.

Stewardship includes the dedication of our talents, our substance, ourselves, even our potential to the Lord. It becomes a vehicle for God to use our lives and our possessions to help others. Stewardship should never be considered a burden. Great joy comes to the steward who prayerfully plans his sharing in a way that will do the most good for the most people.

Far too many of us think no further than tithing when we consider stewardship. Tithing is of vital importance, and failing to tithe is actually stealing from God. However, tithing is but a grain of sand on the stewardship beach. Our time is as important as our material goods—and there is *always* time for anything the Lord wants us to do.

Our homes are part of our stewardship. Whether our house is being used as an activity center for thirty teenagers, or as a haven for a battered wife and her two terror-stricken children, we can be exercising our stewardship to its utmost. *"Inasmuch as ye have done it unto the least of these my brethren, ye have done it unto me"* (Matt. 25:40) applies to either. The size of the crowd is not important; the size of our heart is.

As we open our *heart* to the people God brings to our doorstep, we must open our *door* to them also. A selfish man's house is his "castle," a fortress that shields him from the needs of others. But the unselfish person, the one whose heart is the castle of the King of kings, does not dwell in a barred stockade. Instead, his house is a refuge, a hospice, a cafeteria, an infirmary, a church—ready to meet whatever need of soul or body a visitor might bring.

The steward of such a house prays, "O Lord, bless my home, but, Lord, help me also to *use* it."

CHAPTER FOURTEEN

MOVING TO A NEW HOME

*"For my thoughts are not your thoughts,
neither are your ways my ways, saith the Lord."*
Isaiah 55:8

Although some people are restless, wherever they are, it is not always discontent that causes ours to be a society on the move. Among other reasons, corporations transfer their employees to other cities—or even countries; doctors prescribe other climates for their patients; older people move to areas which will give them a better environment for retirement.

Should you eventually move, for whatever reason, search for a deeper, God-planned reason beyond change of employment, health, or retirement. For God is never haphazard in His planning.

One of the best examples of this is found in the story of Joseph, whose brothers sold him to Midianite traders for twenty pieces of silver. But in Genesis 39:2, we read that *"the Lord was with Joseph."* Later, because Joseph would not be disloyal to his Egyptian master or to God, he was thrown into prison. Yet had not all this happened, Joseph's father and brothers would have starved during the famine in Canaan. Therefore, when reunited with his brothers, Joseph declares, *"...it was not you that sent me hither, but God..."* (Gen. 45:8). He recognized God's sovereignty, even in his enslavement and imprisonment.

If you move, I strongly recommend that you duplicate as many as possible of the features you liked in your former home. In our Arkansas home, we used in many rooms wallpaper identical to that in our former New York home. Our curtains had hung at our New York window for ten years, but we had enough of the same fabric left to make both bedspread and curtains for the master bedroom in our present home. In New York our walls were painted yellow striéd; in Arkansas, they are the same pineapple yellow, but in straw wall covering. Such repetition in design is especially important for children and their adjustment, but it furnishes a warm welcome for the adults in the family, as well.

There are other advantages in duplicating your former design scheme. For one, you will have to expend minimal time or mental energy to redesign the new home. Since the colors and materials have been established, all you need do is decide their configuration.

Also, you will be able to save money. You will not have to replace or recover much furniture.

Finally, because your new home will have quickly conformed to an expression of your family's personality, you will feel "at home" in less time than you would have otherwise. And you will be eager and free to invite and entertain new acquaintances.

CHAPTER FIFTEEN

FOR OLDER HOMEMAKERS

"The righteous...shall still bring forth fruit in their old age."
Psalm 92:14

It has been estimated that 23 percent of the world's greatest achievements have been made by people between the ages of 70 and 80. Unfortunately, however, our western culture is strongly youth-oriented. The majority of marketing programs are aimed at young people; newspapers, magazines, books and television all seem geared to give an older adult the impression that *"Nothing I think, say, or do seems really to matter anyway."*

But this is only our present society's misguided and inappropriate judgment. This was not true of other generations and cultures. And it is certainly not true from Scripture and from God's point of view. One is never too old to be improving, stretching and growing mentally, emotionally and spiritually. A positive attitude toward yourself, your friends, and your surroundings will help to strengthen and expand your inner resources.

So the point I am making here is that it is not too late for you to embark on a good interior design plan for your home. You will no doubt by now have surrounded yourself with comfortable and well-loved pieces in furniture and accessories. Most likely all you need from me is some direction in organization and arrangement. A touch of new paint or wallpaper, some rearranging of furniture, may be just the thing to freshen your home decorating and tie it all together.

Even for those of you who may not be contemplating major changes in your home's interior design, I suggest you begin with the first step of collecting pictures from magazines for a file. You may be pleasantly surprised at the ideas and suggestions which take shape from your analysis.

Of course, to those of you who may be retired and have abilities in various crafts such as needlework, sewing, painting, etc., please let me encourage you to continue to use your skills. Something handmade by you is a loving legacy to family and friends; these kinds of gifts say *"I care"* far more than any mere money can buy.

We can learn from Toyohike Kagawa, the great Japanese Christian: "Though my muscles stiffen, though my skin wrinkle, may I never find myself yawning at life." Longfellow put it in verse:

> *"Chaucer at Woodstock*
> *with the nightingales*
> *At sixty wrote the Canterbury*
> *tales;*
> *Goethe at Weimar, toiling*
> *to the last,*
> *Completed Faust when*
> *eighty years were passed."*

So don't be afraid of growing old. And don't be afraid of change. If you are vaguely dissatisfied with some aspects of your home, you have as good a chance as your daughter of putting good interior design principles to work for yourself!

And a reminder to all of us that the interior-design journey should begin with the Master Designer himself. "Good interior design" for both an individual and a home requires a few basic principles, strong goals, careful planning and faithful maintenance.

PORTFOLIO

Georg Andersen

ASID

Note the use of a number of patterns. The large floral chintz pattern on the sofas, which lends an English country air, and the various patterned oriental rugs work together harmoniously in

spite of what might otherwise appear to be conflicting patterns.

Corner of a living room in a Scarsdale, New York, house with Ethan Allen furniture designed and photographed for use in the **ETHAN ALLEN TREASURY.**

The dining room of an English-style house in Scarsdale, New York, furnished with Ethan Allen furniture.

The living room of the Scarsdale, New York, home also using furnishings from Ethan Allen.

The library of the Scarsdale, New York, house, furnished with Ethan Allen furniture.

The living room in the West Penthouse of the New York Hilton. Note the Bessarabian needlepoint rug.

The dining room of the New York Hilton Penthouse.

The living room in the Greenwich, Connecticut, country house.

The library in the Greenwich, Connecticut, house.

The entrance to the Greenwich, Connecticut, home which is full of lovely antiques.

Marble and other smooth surfaces set the tone in this Harrison, New York, living room. Note the marble-like shading picked up in the carpe●

A Fifth Avenue, New York, apartment living room. Note the "Katrina" wool dhurrie rug designed by Georg Andersen.

The living room of a Sun Valley, Idaho, ski condominium.

The lobby of the Hampshire House in New York. Note the painted, marbleized walls.

A colorful, contemporary living room in a Harrison, New York, residence. Note the multi-colored, ribbon-lacquered screen hiding a giant-screen TV.

A light, airy dining room in a country home from Greenwich, Connecticut.

APPENDIXES

A Case History

Before Mrs. C. H. began her interior-design journey, she asked her husband about his preferences. He said only that he liked well-lit, uncrowded rooms.

When she collected the suggested 40 to 50 pictures of rooms she liked, she settled for 46 that she would use in her analysis. At first she was inclined to pass by those with obviously expensive furnishings. Then she changed her mind. For once she was not going to be unduly concerned with budget; she was simply trying to find out what she really liked.

Since home magazines are expensive, Mrs. C. H. checked with friends for old copies (the manager of her beauty shop gave her several); she found a few in a used bookstore, a few more at a yard sale; she also spotted a few pictures in sales brochures from department stores. Before she bought any magazine, she glanced through it to be sure it had pictures she could use.

Later, when she examined her collection, she had questions about six of the pictures. Why had she included them? she wondered. Analyzing each picture carefully—and making notes on them—Mrs. C. H. became aware that she had saved one picture, not because she especially liked it, but because the living room was like that of a friend she loved. Other pictures were saved because of: a leather-strapped trunk at the foot of a bed, old grocery-store scales on a coffee table, a fluffy kitten curled sleepily on a sofa, an unusual arrangement of books in an arched niche.

Then there was the picture of a breakfast-room table draped in a strawberry-print cloth—of no especial interest; but a captivating teddy bear, with a matching, strawberry-print napkin tied around his neck, was seated at the table. That did it! A stuffed toy; a fluffy kitten; old trunks or scales—none of these may be a good basis for interior-design planning. But at least Mrs. C. H. knew why she'd kept each picture. And those things could possibly stimulate her imagination in adopting novel ideas of her own.

Several pictures of rooms were what Mrs. C. H. called "almosts." One living room contained white wicker chairs and sofa. She liked the furniture, but for some unknown reason, she knew she wouldn't like it in her living room.

The floral print of bluebells draped on a dining table seemed attractive. But matched in the overcurtains, the wallpaper, and the chair cushions, it was a bit much. Other "almosts" were: a sofa in a pink, white and green, but a too-large floral pattern; a blue-bordered rug with a blue-gray seashell design on a beige background; a gray-bordered rug with a geometric—almost Oriental—pattern.

Mrs. C. H. was *sure* she would like to include in her plans a pictured dining room of blond wood with a glass-front china closet in darker wood (or the colors could be reversed). She was sure. But she then saw the beautiful, overstuffed host and hostess chairs in the blue-and-white brocade, with matching cushions on the side chairs. Her confusion pushed her to search for an answer. Of course! The interior design of her home, like other worthwhile things, would certainly "grow" and change. So, why not keep one of the pictures for possible consideration in her future plans?

What did Mrs. C. H. learn about herself by analyzing those 46 pictures? Probably the most important lesson was to be tolerant of, to see redeeming features in, interior-design plans that others liked—even ones that she personally did not care for. Because she felt an exciting, vicarious pleasure upon seeing some of the pictures, she learned, too, that she need not *own* beautiful things in order to enjoy them.

Mrs. C. H. confirmed, rather than learned, that she liked rooms with plenty of light—white priscilla curtains in bedrooms. Her favorite color is blue, with pink a close runner-up. Splashes of coral and dabs of accent in green, red, and yellow please her, as does the green of growing plants. Unfortunately, she has a "brown thumb," but she is trying to work with hardy plants, such as wandering jew, spider plant and aloe vera.

Reasonably happy with the cinnamon-colored, wall-to-wall carpeting in her present bedroom and hall, Mrs. C. H. knows that when it is time to change, she will opt for blue or green. In living room and dining room, she likes warm-brown floors. One picture showed a perfect rug for her dining room: a blue-gray border with a design of tiny leaves, scattered in oval patterns on a beige background.

Should Mrs. C. H. choose wallpaper or paint? Since her budget is limited, she will probably settle for paint. If some wallpaper can be managed, it will be a tiny floral design, probably on a white background.

Two rooms, captioned as a French drawing room and dining room, each as large as our case historian's entire house, were regal but completely out of her financial reach or her needs. Still, she is pleased to have seen their beauty. A kitchen, as rustic as the other rooms were regal, brought a momentary longing (or was it nostalgia?) for an old flour barrel used as a chair, a brick floor, and a fireplace bellows. Her longing, too, was momentary.

She could almost taste the salty brine from an old pickle crock. Two "Regulator" school clocks, a parade drum used as a coffee table, a bird cage refinished in shining simulated silver, fall-dried tumbleweeds scattered about a living room—all fascinated her.

Since one idea begets another, Mrs. C. H. knew she would put her antique sewing machine in the guest bedroom to be used as an end table. Those old brass picture frames, polished to a high gloss, would be perfect for turn-of-the-century landscape paintings. That appliqued butterfly quilt her sister made for her would look great hanging from their bedroom wall....

Budget-Cutting Ideas

1. Wallpaper rooms with a pattern that will reduce—or eliminate—the need for wall decorations. For instance, let a floral design provide your family and your guests with a simulated bouquet or garden. Such a room requires only the simplest curtains, or none at all.

Should you question the wisdom of buying wallpaper for a rented apartment, consider the length of time you will live there. Then decide whether the pleasure of such surroundings is worth the expense.

2. To get the most interior-design mileage, use simplicity to put the "right accent on the right syllable." If room colors are all neutral, bring compatible color into the room in: good lamps; lacquered coffee tables; frames around mirrors; curtain treatment (if the room has only one window or two well-balanced windows); and frames or seats of a pair of open-arm chairs. Keep your centers of interest to a minimum, thus avoiding a cluttered appearance.

3. Instead of buying a large area rug, say, 14' × 16', buy less expensive wall-to-wall carpeting and place a smaller area rug over it, such as a 6' × 9' or even a 4' × 6'.

4. One way of having a luxurious look in your room, without spending a great deal of money, is to build your color scheme around the colors of the print in a fabric, known as a *lead fabric*. The background color is the basic color of your scheme. If you can afford enough for only one or two throw pillows, they will add a look of richness to the entire room. Use the lesser colors in the print to complement the scheme.

5. When buying a sofa, settle for having it covered in a less-expensive fabric. Then buy more expensive fabric for throw pillows.

6. Instead of buying furnishings in a rush with the chance that they may not please you later, make your selections carefully. This is especially true in regard to modern furniture. Focus on simple pieces that will fit into many different schemes and that will be adaptable over the years. For instance, the simplest four-drawer chest, 48" wide by 18" deep by 32" or 36" high, will fit into many rooms and serve many functions. On the other hand, a 7'-long dresser may become obsolete at the first rearrangement of furniture or at the first move to another home.

7. I advise people who are buying furniture of substance or worth to consider a more classic design, such as "authentic" copies of English or French furniture. Avoid tricky variations or adaptations of today's general commercial furniture.

8. Purchase that smaller-scale sofa, 6' to 7' long. It will cost less, use less fabric and be easier to fit into almost any situation.

9. Put your money where it will count the most—not in small, expensive accessories (which, in truth, are "extras") but rather in that simply designed but well-made coffee table.

10. Don't attempt to discard everything you have and start over. Reevaluate—perhaps the sofa print doesn't match the curtain print, but take another look at those curtains. Maybe adding a contrasting ruffle to them will give them a fresh look and give you money to spend for something else in the room.

Recently, for practical reasons, we added ruffles to a client's existing curtains. They were too short, hanging 3" off the floor. The new ruffle gave the curtains the added length they needed and accented one of the colors that existed in the print.

Throw Pillows

Ideally, throw pillows should be knife-edged without a welt. Unless a family member is allergic, splurge and use throw pillows of 100 percent down. My rationale for using down is that it is very soft and adds an inviting look to any sofa or chair. If making your own pillows, buy sanitized down already in the proper-sized casing from a reputable upholsterer.

This pillow has shirred or Turkish corners, made by pulling the ''ears'' of the pillow inside (a more formal look).

Pillows of these styles look best from 19½'' square to 22'' square. Cord trim can be inserted in the seams for a dressier appearance. Use tassel trim only for a very period room.

An excellent throw-pillow size for a traditional room is 18'' square. Use a smaller pillow only if it's centered on the back of a sofa or chair—then 12'' × 16'' is good. A size smaller than this appears insignificant and does not give you enough for your money.

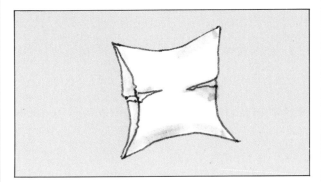

This pillow is square at the corners (a less formal look).

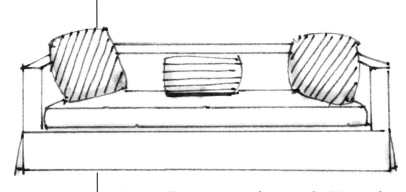

Throw pillows positioned on a sofa. Notice the smaller, rectangular one at the center.

INDEXES

INDEX OF INTERIOR-DESIGN COMPONENTS

INDEX OF INTERIOR-DESIGN COMPONENTS

Color	Manufacturer	Paint No.	Page
Apple Green	Sherwin Williams	BM 24-20	33
	Pittsburgh Paints	M3000	
	Benjamin Moore	GR-52	
Bottle Green	Sherwin Williams	BM 28-31	27
	Pittsburgh Paints	N 7004	
	Benjamin Moore	AJ-55	
Navy	Sherwin Williams	BM 32-24	27
	Pittsburgh Paints	N 7062	
	Benjamin Moore	PV-61	
Neutra	Sherwin Williams	EX BM 3-11	20
	Pittsburgh Paints	P 2635	
	Benjamin Moore	CB-41	
Pineapple	Sherwin Williams	BM 19-1	33
	Pittsburgh Paints	P 2307	
	Benjamin Moore	YL-18	
Raspberry	Sherwin Williams	BM 1-31	27
	Pittsburgh Paints	N 7157	
	Benjamin Moore	PR-37	
Robin's Egg Blue	Sherwin Williams	BM 32-25	20
	Pittsburgh Paints	P 2071	
	Benjamin Moore	AJ-24	
Tangerine	Sherwin Williams	BM 8-23	33
	Pittsburgh Paints	N 7189	
	Benjamin Moore	OP-61	
Terra Cotta	Sherwin Williams	BM 7-23	20
	Pittsburgh Paints	D 4240	
	Benjamin Moore	ST-38	

Armoire	Usually a large and ornate cupboard, wardrobe, or clothespress.
Bobeches	Glass discs that hold candle drippings.
Cozy corner	A large or small section of a room, conducive to relaxing with family or friends, or being alone.
Dacron nylon	A tightly woven sheer fabric, used for under-curtains.
Dhurrie rug	A thin, flat, woven rug; reversible and made of either wool or cotton; woven in India or locally by hand. Most of the new dhurries are made of wool. Little is known about their origin—a dhurrie that is fifty years or older is considered an antique and will always be cotton.
Down lighting	Any lighting installed in or on the ceiling.
Etagere	A cabinet consisting of a tier of open shelves.
Floor-can lamps	Cylindrical or square fixtures which sit on the floor (often used in corners or behind indoor plants). Their light shines upward toward the ceiling.
Focal point	A center of activity or visual interest.
Formal painting	Usually one from a certain period of history; has recognizable scenes or objects.
Foyer	An entrance hallway.
Harp (for lamp)	A metal hoop or arch that supports a lamp shade.
Heirlooms	"Treasures of the heart"
Hurricane lamps	A lamp with a glass chimney placed over a candle to keep it from being blown out by the wind.
Kilim rug	A thin, flat, woven, reversible rug, made of fine quality wool, and usually woven in Hungary by hand. Kilims differ from Dhurries in that their weave is much finer, allowing for considerably more intricate designs.
Loveseat	A small sofa not longer than 66" (5'6").
Overcurtains	Commonly called draperies.
Primitives (paintings)	These can be American or, as often is the case, from less-developed regions such as Haiti. Always *very* colorful and simplistic; they are painted in a flat style with little consideration of perspective (a principle of drawing which gives a sense of depth).
Rheostat	A resistor for measuring currents by means of variable resistances (another word for dimmer).
Sconce	A bracket candlestick, or group of candlesticks.
Series lighting	Similar to the wiring principle of old-fashioned Christmas-tree lighting, but with white bulbs.

Settee	A small sofa not longer than 66" (5'6") usually on legs and quite often with an exposed wooden frame.
Strié	A striped design used especially in textiles that consists of faint, streaked vertical lines of color, close in tone to the background.
Style space	Area between two equally proportioned pictures hanging side by side. Not a good arrangement because it confuses the eye.
Swatchboard	A base, such as heavy cardboard, that holds samples of fabric, carpeting, wallpaper and paint. Each sample should be in proportion to the area of the room it represents.
Terra cotta	A pale rust color.
Tôle	A decorative painted tin, or other metal, finished in various colors.

Undercurtains	Such curtains are used behind overcurtains (draperies), acting as a "slip" to give the window a finished effect.
Valance	A heading of wood or metal to frame or to conceal the tops of curtains and fixtures.
Vitrine	A glass showcase for display of fine wares or specimens.
Votive candle	A candle that, when lighted, is intended by some to express a vow, desire, or prayer; we use them decoratively.
Wall-washer lights	These can be recessed in the ceiling or mounted on the ceiling. These lighting fixtures will cast light downward at an angle, illuminating a wall or painting more dramatically than an ordinary down light.

Adams, Jay E., *Christian Living in the Home,* Presbyterian and Reformed Publishing Company; Phillipsburg, New Jersey; 1979

Allen, Charles L., *Life More Abundant,* Fleming H. Revell Company; Old Tappan, New Jersey; 1977

Andersen, Georg, *Scrapbook*

Christensen, Larry & Nordis, *The Christian Couple,* Bethany House Publishers; Minneapolis; 1977

Deen, Edith, *Family Living in the Bible,* Harper & Row Publishers, Inc.; New York; 1963

Dobson, Dr. James C., *Straight Talk to Men and Their Wives*; Word Book Publisher; Waco, Texas; 1980

Fagan, A. R., *What the Bible Says about Stewardship*; Convention Press; Nashville; 1979

Gaither, Gloria, *Because He Lives,* Fleming H. Revell Company; Old Tappan, New Jersey; 1977

Greer, Michael, *Inside Design,* Doubleday & Company, Inc.; New York; 1962

Haskins, Dorothy C., *God in My Home,* Warner Press; Anderson, Indiana; 1973

Kurtz, Kenneth, *Wooden Chalices,* The Bethany Press; St. Louis; 1963

LaHaye, Tim & Bev, *Spirit-Controlled Family Living,* Fleming H. Revell Company; Old Tappan, New Jersey; 1978

Mains, Karen Burton, *Open Heart—Open Home*; David C. Cook Publishing Company; Elgin, Illinois; 1976

McKay, Charles, *The Spirit-Filled Steward*; Convention Press; Nashville; 1974

Myers, T. Cecil, *Happiness Is Still Home Made*; Word Books Incorporated; 1972

Speer, Michael L., *A Complete Guide to the Christian's Budget*; Broadman Press; Nashville; 1975

Taylor, Robert S., *The Disciplined Life-Style*; Bethany House Publishers; 1981

Tozer, A. W., *Who Put Jesus on the Cross*; Christian Publications, Inc., Harrisburg, Pennsylvania; 1975